# OLYMPIC WANDERING

*Time Travel Through Greece*

David Lundberg

Zante

ZANTE

Illustrations by
Lauren Matthews & Erin Farney

Cover design by Karen Ross

ISBN  0-9763246-4-4

Library of Congress Control Number
2004098371


First Printing 2005

# Acknowledgments

I am indebted to the Greek poet Homer for his *Iliad* and *Odyssey,* and to the many modern translations of both works in addition to the various adaptations to film. I am also grateful to my sister, Chris Young, my daughter Erica, and my friend Dr. Jerry Juhnke for their helpful comments regarding the early manuscript.

Finally, to the people of Greece, past, present and future, I extend my respect and affection.

*To*

*Vasso, Paul, Erica & Steve*

*You've given me so much through time*

# Introduction

Our airliner descended through wet, gray clouds on final approach to the Athens International Airport. It was early April and raining.

The clinging mist slipped above the plane. Below us white, box-like homes and apartments flowed toward the sea like speckled lava from a smoldering eruption. In years to come I learned that the core of this volcano was the pulsating, central city of Athens. Since the middle of the twentieth century it had swollen to critical mass, pushing out in all directions, making Greece one of the most lop-sided countries in the world. In a country of ten million souls nearly half lived in Athens.

The airliner bounced on the runway and slowed. The engines screamed for a few moments then faded as the plane veered toward terminal buildings. We ground to a stop. My fellow passengers rose, sluggish from ten hours of cramped sitting and shuffled toward the exit door as fresh air rushed inside to greet us. We descended a wheeled staircase and climbed into a blue airport bus.

The hills around us sprouted billboards with strange-looking phrases advertising cigarettes, soft drinks and cars. Half the letters looked familiar. The other half were like symbols from a high school physics book or the sign on a college fraternity house.

Stopping in front of the main building, the bus doors opened and we stumbled out. The wide marble steps of the terminal entrance seemed too elaborate for a simple commercial building. Inside, floors of smooth terrazzo gave rise to vertical steel beams framing walls of plate glass. Sunlight filtered in, casting soft shadows. The tired voices of travelers bounced around.

Weary and disoriented, we lined up at immigration control. The line inched forward, and each person prepared to volunteer a passport. The little booklets came in dark, serious colors. Navy blue, forest green, maroon.

The blue-uniformed fellow behind the counter was a study in supreme boredom. He transmitted an attitude of complete indifference that had to be the result of intensive training. Inspecting my passport with a placid face, he flipped until mysteriously satisfied, stamped a random page and handed it back, making sure not to look at me. With a bored expression he waved the back of his hand in the general direction of the baggage area. His glazed eyes glanced at the next body moving toward him. After the briefest eye contact, he repeated the entire procedure without deviation.

I picked up my suitcase and walked through double doors into the reception area. It was a noisy sea of faces, each person's gaze streaming past me searching for friends or relatives from the plane. With a look of recognition a pale American stepped forward and shook my hand. Most of the olive-skinned men surrounding us had their shirts unbuttoned halfway. Each fellow sported a neck chain with a simple gold cross nearly buried in a mass of dark chest hair. They smoked pungent, unfiltered cigarettes.

Outside the rain had stopped, and sunlight shot down and attacked my eyes. This light was different, - brilliant and soft. It wrapped around objects and made them glow. The edges of things were very distinct. Arriving in Greece is like entering a dark room at night, turning on the lights, and putting on your glasses all at once.

The main colors were deep blue and pure white. Blue sea and white boats. Blue sky and white clouds. Blue uniforms and airport buses. White houses and apartments. The white objects were sources of brilliant, reflected illumination. The dark blue formed a stark contrast in a land bathed in liquid light.

My driver chattered away as his beat-up car labored up an incline to the main street. He tried to convince me of the importance of my new job, but I barely heard him.

Cars hurtled by at odd angles and dramatically changing speeds. We eased to a stop at a traffic light just *after* it turned red. Stopping on yellow was an invitation to be rear-ended. Drivers expended a great deal of emotional energy during the transitions of traffic lights from one color to another. In the millisecond just *before* a light changed from red to green, any motorist who did not anticipate that change and inch into the intersection, was promptly prodded by a chorus of complaining horns.

Likewise there was an overwhelming desire to speed up and escape through an intersection *just after* the light turned from yellow to red. The sweet victory of an able driver.

The transitions between traffic lanes were meaningless. Two clearly marked lanes going in one direction were transformed into three or even four lines of cars, making use of every fraction of road width. If any space opened between the lines of autos, that area was explosively consumed by young, almost suicidal motorcyclists who weaved through traffic with great daring and skill.

Greek traffic has a strict pecking order. The biggest and most powerful vehicle has absolute priority. A large Mercedes has precedence over a small Ford. A big truck preempts the Mercedes. If a larger vehicle traveling in the same direction is alongside and the nose of that vehicle is slightly ahead, your lane of traffic is his for the taking. He may cut into your lane at will, and you must yield to higher gross weight and horsepower.

After a mile or two of this automotive circus the road dead-ended at the sea. We turned and followed the coastal highway past hotels, restaurants and apartments. The hotels had strangely mixed names: *The Congo Palace, The Albatross, Le Bonavista*. Red and white blossoms burst from laurel bushes growing out of dirt and weeds in the highway median.

It was mid-morning and the streets buzzed. Every restaurant had outside tables, but the customers hadn't ordered much. Iced coffee, perhaps a small snack.

A huge bay swept around on the right, sprinkled with small, gently rocking fishing boats. It was mid-week, but plenty of people were on the beach and in the water. Our car topped a crest, and another bay ringed with yachts lay directly ahead. A sign proclaiming *"Astir Beach"* hung over a large, cabana-like structure. A sharp turn took us to one of those oddly named hotels, "*The Margi House*." A boxy building with a simple, elegant façade.

The driver dropped me off, saw that I was checked in and motored away. I deposited my suitcase in a sparsely furnished room and took the hotel elevator to the rooftop restaurant. A waiter ushered me to an outside table, and I ordered something called *moussaka* having no clue what it was. Powerful yachts skidded across the bay, the breeze drifted in, the sunshine was blinding.

The next three years of my life became a series of wonderful incidents. I lived through a time that resembled an exotic foreign movie. My viewing screen was panoramic, a 360-degree theater of sights, sounds and attitudes that changed my life forever.

Greeks are wedded to the waters. Understanding them begins where the sea embraces the land ... the fabulous Greek isles.

# Islands, Gods, and People

The gods ordained this country for individualism. The geography demands it. Greece is a ragged bag of precious stones spilled across the eastern Mediterranean. Frayed mountains march defiantly and sink into the sea, reemerging later as gem-like islands of different size, character and brilliance. This is an arid, rugged country of forty thousand square miles with nine thousand miles of shoreline. Over three-quarters of the people live in coastal areas.

Counts of the islands vary like estimates of the population of Athens. Ask several natives how many people live in the capital city, and you receive distinct authoritative replies ranging between four and six million. Some reference books state there are one thousand islands. Some say three thousand or more. It just depends how well you can count all the large and small rocks that emerge from Greek waters.

Holding five large islands, the Ionian Sea bathes the shores of western Greece. On the other side of the country, over fifty well-inhabited isles float in the Aegean Sea as it washes the beaches of the east coast. Crete is the southernmost island, forming a natural boundary between Greek waters and the Mediterranean Sea. Crete is a large rectangular land of over three thousand square miles. Because of its size and long rich history, it is a world unto itself.

This is a land of rampant individuality within a strong cultural framework. When you meet a Greek two things stand out. First, bursting vitality confronts you. This nation is a celebration of life, and the people have an energy that is startling. Second, you sense a person with a strong, almost overpowering, sense of self.

On one of our return visits to Athens my wife and I tried a little experiment. When we caught a taxi we engaged the driver in conversation, and after a few minutes of pleasant banter we asked the cabby his opinion of the current political leader.

If we rode in twenty taxis during that visit, it seemed like we received twenty totally different responses to our question. Each reply was delivered with confidence and a unique perspective, as if each person described a different politician.

That type of passionate diversity is very Greek. It's as if imitation is considered shallow, lazy or inferior. Personal independence is a strong cultural value, and perhaps that helps explain why this country was the birthplace of democracy.

Five thousand years ago western civilization sprouted in the Middle East, and it moved in the direction of the setting sun. After Mesopotamia and Sumeria, Egypt became the next great power followed by Greece, Rome, Western Europe and finally, the Americas.

In *The Greek Way* Edith Hamilton describes the clear distinction between ancient Greece and neighboring lands. Prior civilizations were dictatorial and miserable for the common person. A few powerful despots ruled, and they treated other human beings as property of little value. Slavery was widespread, the people had little hope and death was often preferable to life. Religion was magical and fearful, the special domain of priests who served the kings while those rulers subjugated the people. The emphasis of those cultures was on death. Life wasn't all that pleasant.

In a land of invigorating weather and beautiful islands the people we know as Greeks emerged and turned the world upside down. Their emphasis was on life. Their gods were like passionate mortals, and the people were like gods, just not as powerful. Their world was a continuum of greater gods, lesser gods, half-gods and mortals. The gods mixed freely with human beings, and this strongly influenced the legendary hospitality of the Greeks. Any stranger could be a deity in disguise so visitors were treated royally. To this day one of the worst insults you can bestow on a Greek is to say he or she was inhospitable.

The gods and goddesses formed the cast of the world's first great soap opera. They held court on Mount Olympus, the highest mountain in the land, and each of the deities was unique. Every one on Olympus had a special characteristic like love or wisdom, a particular realm like the sea or the underworld, or a personal domain like war or the harvest. But they couldn't mind their own business. The gods and goddesses constantly squabbled, interfering with each other and with human beings. They were like talented rich people with plenty of energy, resources and time on their hands. They inevitably got into a great deal of mischief.

Zeus was king of the mountain, first among his peers and strongest. But he was not all-powerful, and he often sidestepped the intrigue all around him. Meanwhile he hatched schemes of his own, including numerous love affairs with mortals. This exasperated his wife, the goddess Hera. In return she often tried to manipulate her husband, enlisting other gods and goddesses in her plotting.

The intermingling of gods with mortals produced offspring like Achilles and Helen, powerful men and beautiful women.

In a mountainous, island country unity was scarce. City-states developed as isolated self-supporting units, and the people evolved the same way. They believed that each person was independent just as every city-state was autonomous. In a culture where each person felt special humanity rose, producing an era of stunning achievement in art, architecture, science and thought. The world has marveled at it ever since. Buildings like the Parthenon rose as testimonies to universal human brilliance.

In a similar way every Greek island is unique. Today many visitors return to a particular island year after year. It's a heartfelt reunion with a dear friend. It's like coming home.

An island is a true destination. You skim across the sea, and in the distance a piece of land crystallizes. You draw near, and an intimate harbor reaches out and embraces you. Walking around, you feel a bond with individuals who belong to this isolated place.

Islands invite intimacy. They seduce you. It is impossible to know many people well, but you can know one person or one island very well. You enter into a manageable, personal relationship and if compatible, it becomes a long-term love affair.

Like a young man in the first flush of full adult powers, the island of Ithaca rises confidently from the Ionian Sea. Energetic, aggressive, naively self-assured. Curving alongside Ithaca is the much larger island of Cephalonia. Lush, fertile and mother-like. Cephalonia half-circles and almost embraces Ithaca like a well-endowed mother hovering over a grown son who needs no protection.

The relationship of a Greek mother with her independent adult sons is very close. They are the center of her universe, and she makes that attitude clear. Little wonder those sons grow willful and capable, each one believing innately that the world revolves around him.

Three thousand years ago the poet Homer wrote the first great works of western literature. The *Iliad* describes the Trojan War; the *Odyssey* outlines the struggle of Odysseus, known in the west as Ulysses, in his struggle to return home after the war.

In those ancient times dramatic storytellers like Homer passed on grand legends. Acute minds developed in a different way, memorizing long tales in poetic form. In the evenings around a banquet table and warm fire, these bards entertained hungry, willing audiences. They narrated great drama. Battles, love affairs, everyday life, and extraordinary life. But best of all they described people. Their cares, their joys, their triumphs, their defeats. And the people they pictured were indelibly Greek, just as they are today.

Ithaca was the home Ulysses longed for during twenty years of war and wandering. He had a relationship with his island that transcended wife, children or parents. It was a vital part of who he was. As long as he was absent he was fragmented. Only on Ithaca was he complete.

When Ulysses returned he was weathered and aged. He had survived ten years of conflict, aiding in the conquest of a great power, ancient Troy. He then spent another ten years struggling to get home through storms, shipwreck and captivity. During his long absence he faced every conceivable challenge. It was all preparation for what awaited him. Over one hundred envious suitors had swarmed his palace, taking advantage of natural Greek hospitality to besiege Ulysses' wife.

He had lost his entire fleet, not a single person returned with him. His only chance to regain his life lay in patience, cunning and strength. In the end he secretly engaged his son, two faithful shepherds and an old nurse. Disguised as a beggar he infiltrated the palace, used the same trick of hospitality, maneuvered the complacent suitors into positions of vulnerability and struck without mercy.

Like Ulysses the Greek people have survived and triumphed over tremendous odds. The story of Ulysses strangely foreshadows the history of the Greeks.

The language of Homer was rich and extensive, but his style of writing was simple. And as Hamilton points out, he wrote the way Greeks looked at the world, in terms of simple beauty. They didn't use flowery adjectives to stimulate their emotions. What they saw, felt and heard was enough. Life was so rich it didn't need decoration.

The *Odyssey* is a long, classic, narrative poem that is not easy to read. It describes places in ancient, forgotten names. The many characters appear and reappear without warning. Their names are long and complex.

In *Prospero's Cell* Lawrence Durrell notes that the ancient *Odyssey* describes one thing with "delightful and poignant accuracy" ... the modern Greeks. Cunning, resourceful, noble, devious, loyal, treacherous, constantly vacillating between extremes and always assertive, the people Homer pictured are mirrored today in the current occupants of this land. In the midst of Homer's description stands Ulysses. At first glance there is nothing special about him. The gods, half-gods and other kings are all more attractive. Dark red hair and beard frame his plain face. He is less than average height, short-legged and walks with a slight limp, the result of a boyhood hunting accident. But veiled behind this humble exterior is the ultimate hero of the *Iliad* and the *Odyssey*.

Beneath loose robes lies a finely balanced and powerful body. He is well muscled with massive chest, strong arms and powerful thighs. Ulysses is an excellent boxer, wrestler and sprinter, an expert with bow, sword and spear. He is the ancient equivalent of a modern decathlon champion.

Hidden behind that common face lies a brilliant mind. He is stunningly eloquent and persuasive. His highly disciplined will is focused, and his intelligence rules. He makes no emotional mistakes therefore he acts with assurance. His creative mind is always framing some new craftiness.

He is a daring master of disguise who uses deception to defeat his enemies. Dressed as a poor tramp he walks straight into the Trojan camp then into the city of Troy itself, talking with Helen, gathering information and returning undetected. In his most famous trick he hides his men inside a huge wooden horse and sends the rest of the army away. The Trojans drag the horse within their walls, the Greeks emerge at night, and Troy falls.

Ulysses is proud, but he has no false vanity. He can plow a field, tend a vineyard, sail a ship or defeat an army. He is a magnificent leader, known as the ravager of cities. Yet his own people describe him as the kindest and gentlest of men. In battle he is a savage butcher, but when one of his own men falls in combat, he weeps.

If the island of Ithaca is like a son and Cephalonia a close and nearly inseparable mother, the isle of Lefkas to the north is like a father. Lefkas is a bit distant from Ithaca just as fathers are sometimes less intimate with sons. It is a large strong island. Lefkas is simple, almost peasant-like, but has unexpected beauty. Magnificent mountains, wild winds, and proud people.

The final isle in Ulysses' realm was Zakynthos. It lies to the south of the other three islands, further away, almost like it belongs to another family. Zakynthos is blooming and fragrant, the warmest and most musical of the Ionians, a place of romance.

These islands formed the kingdom over which Ulysses reigned. Ithaca contained his palace. From the smallest of the major Ionian isles he looked out over a rich deep sea.

Travel back in time into the life of Ulysses. Not primarily the Trojan War, which took place outside modern Greece. And not mainly the Odyssey. That happened mostly beyond Greek waters. Follow Ulysses through the seldom-told tale of his journey within Greece itself.

Then come with me as I trace that same path today. In the distant past we look forward over the centuries to the present time. In today's world we gaze back through the scenes of history.

The islands, the people and the spirit of the gods endure, and we become part of it.

Corfu

Skiathos

Skyros

Lefkas

Chalkis

Ithaca

Aulis

Egion

Cephalonia

Corinth

Aegina

Zakynthos

Spetses

*Part One*

# At Home

Ulysses emerged dripping from the sea. Behind him the morning sun peeked over mountains on the mainland. Drops on his skin glistened red in the morning light. He walked to a large rock where his cloth lay and sponged off.

His parents had raised him bluntly. His father Laertes challenged him physically, emotionally, but most of all mentally, teaching him to think creatively no matter what problem arose. If you bargained in the market, you changed words and tactics to unbalance the merchant. When you boxed or wrestled you moved when your opponent least expected it. Often a wrestling match turned when an adversary hesitated over a surprising tactic, and the victory was yours.

Laertes said, "Son, we are a passionate people, but mistakes come from the passions. If you act from brash confidence, fear or anger, you give your opponent a chance to drive in the sword. Above all, think! Use alternating, even strange methods. Never stupid, emotional ones."

"You must outwit, out-trick and outfight any challenger. A proud person may think his intelligence or skill as a boxer will be enough. If he is good he will win often, but he will eventually fall to the person who uses trickery or a bold, careful lie."

"Father, you're not a liar."

"Ulysses, your mother's father, Autolycus, was a strong and able man. He was also a great liar, and I learned some things from him. I am good and fair and honest with most people. But if someone is deceitful or dishonest I surprise him with his own tricks. He doesn't expect them from me."

"The gods look with favor on you. You are a king."

Laertes paused to get a different angle on the yoke he was carving. "The gods favor those who win."

That moment in his father's workshop seemed like yesterday, but Laertes was older now and Ulysses was king. Thirty years old, at the height of his physical and mental powers. Two years ago he had married. Two months ago his first child was born.

When young princes chose a wife location was primary. If an alliance was struck with the home realm of a bride, power expanded. Physical beauty was important, wisdom was valued less and good character assumed. Ulysses turned these values upside down.

First, he limited the selection to his home kingdom. Ulysses realized that power plays and shifting alliances through marriage were based on greed. It was tough enough holding on to what you had, and he had a great deal.

Second, beauty was vain. He watched the princes of Greece vie for the hand of Helen, known as the world's most beautiful woman, coveted on both sides of the Aegean. He observed Helen when she chose Menelaus, king of Sparta. What he saw troubled him. She was willful and proud. Ulysses made a journey to ask for the hand of Helen as did all the other Greek princes. But his heart wasn't in it. In the end he swore a blood-oath of allegiance to Helen. He had little choice. Honor compelled the suitors to defend this prize.

It was a one-sided deal. Ulysses gained nothing by pledging loyalty to another king's bride, and it made him uneasy. Beauty would go lower on his list.

Ulysses finished drying himself and threw a cloak over his shoulders. It was soft and warm, woven of lamb's wool from his flocks. A small sack containing his dagger and some food lay beside the rock. He belted the short sword around his waist, walked toward the hill behind the beach and reached into the bag for some fruit.

There was movement on the top of the rise, and his right hand grabbed for the dagger. A familiar form swept across the ridge and Ulysses relaxed. It was the graceful outline of his friend, Polites.

The two were like brothers. As boys they had taken lessons together and played together. Sometimes they quarreled, but as the years went by childish arguments faded and they became inseparable.

They were both all-around fine athletes. But in one area Polites was clearly superior, ... long distance running. Polites saw his friend, changed direction and started descending the slope.

A shout tumbled down the hill. "Sire! ... Sire!"

Two years ago when Ulysses was anointed king Polites began calling him "Sire" in public. That was the only change in their relationship. When alone all else was the same. Drawing close he slowed to a walk, hands on hips, inhaling deeply.

"You breathe hard, my friend. You're out of shape."

"They come!"

"Menelaus?"

Still out of breath, Polites lowered his eyes and nodded in a single short movement.

Ulysses gazed across the water. "Then the rumors are true. She left with Paris."

"You mean she was kidnapped."

"No. Doesn't make sense. Helen is the most beautiful woman in the world. Heavily guarded. My bet is that for Paris to get her she had to cooperate."

Ulysses spun around, put his hand on his friend's shoulder and they started up the hill. "Polites, Menelaus comes for me. He goes against Troy, and he will muster every good available man. I'm pledged to defend Helen. So here I am, a young king, newly married with a newborn son, forced to join a campaign to retrieve a willful woman who I suspect can't keep her skirts hitched up."

"Well, get out of it!"

"That won't be easy. It's a matter of a sacred pledge, and we are men of honor. A simple refusal is out of the question."

They reached the top of the rise, sun bursting full strength behind them. Ulysses' fortress crowned the highest hill, the best defensive spot on the northern half of Ithaca. But his thoughts roamed far to the east to a grand palace surrounded by nearly impregnable walls ... Troy.

Polites' breathing had returned to normal. "What will you do?"

"I don't know."

"You better think quickly. I doubt you have more than a day or two."

"Thank you, my brother," he said, embracing Polites. "You came quickly."

They separated and Ulysses raised his hand. Polites turned and moved down the path toward his home.

Ulysses entered the gate of the fortress, mind churning. If Helen had not been kidnapped, the kings would have found another reason to go to war with Troy. They had agitated for conflict for years.

The eastern Greeks were powerful merchants led by Agamemnon of Mycenae, brother of Menelaus. Their shipping routes covered the Mediterranean world, and they traded freely in nearly every direction. East to Cyprus and Egypt, north through the Balkans, even south and west to lands Ulysses did not know.

Only Troy challenged the Greek fleet. And they did so in a very profitable market. A narrow channel called the Hellespont provided the only water route from the Aegean to the rich Black Sea. The trade winds blew in a southwesterly direction, straight down this waterway into the Aegean. Troy sat at the entrance to the passage. Most ships traveling past the city-state had to stop and wait for a lull in the winds before proceeding. From its position guarding the waterway, Troy grew rich extracting tolls from the merchants. The more powerful the Trojans became, the more money they demanded.

But Troy's muscle was turning to fat. It had peaked as a superpower, and the Greeks sensed it. Helen's "kidnapping" by a Trojan prince was the break that Agamemnon longed for, a grand excuse to rally his allies against the adversary.

Helen's questionable loyalty to her husband and Mycenaean resentment of taxation were poor reasons for Ulysses to jump into this conflict. During the past two years he had consolidated his father's gains and was ready to hold them against threats.

Threats would come. If Ulysses left for war the challenges would come more quickly, more strongly. The best men would accompany him. He would take the strength of his kingdom far away and leave Ithaca vulnerable.

Once inside the gate he crossed the courtyard and bounded up the marble steps of the palace. His throne room and banquet hall lay directly ahead. He turned and walked up the steps to his son's nursery. Soft singing flowed from the room along with the cooing and gurgling of a happy baby.

Framed against the window, Penelope sat with knees up and her back against the edge of a low sofa. The baby was in her outstretched arms, resting against her knees. The baby looked straight into her eyes, his legs moving in erratic jerks.

Eurycleia, the childhood nurse of Ulysses, sat on a stool. She rose as he drew near. He placed his hand on her delicate shoulder.

"Sire, the child has your eyes and your body."

"Maybe he will have his mother's face."

Penelope stopped singing as Ulysses crouched on the vacant stool. Without looking toward her husband she said, "He is alert and strong. His little mind isn't cluttered yet."

"It will be."

Penelope said, "Cleia, take Telemachus out for some fresh air."

"Yes, my lady." The nurse took the child and departed.

"How did you sleep, my treasure?" Ulysses asked.

"Deeply. How was your swim?"

"Good, ... Menelaus comes."

"Then the stories about Helen are true?"

"They must be."

Penelope spun on the sofa and dropped her feet to the floor. "What will you do?"

"I will do what I must."

"You know what I mean. What will you do with Menelaus?"

He leaned over and kissed her. "I will know when he comes."

Ulysses rose, sliding his hand through his wife's hair. He turned and left the room.

Halfway down the stairs a noisy explosion burst from the kitchen. Metal pots banged against one another and the floor, followed by high-pitched shouts from angry women. Ulysses reached the bottom step and a bent figure sped by, his left hand clutching a loaf of bread.

Ulysses shouted, "Eurybates!"

The hunchback halted, spun toward the steps and straightened up. "At your service, Sire!"

Ulysses closed the distance between them. "Judging from that fresh loaf of bread it appears your service is to your own belly."

"Great King of the Ionians, warrior without equal, master of this realm, my eyes, ears and golden lips are at your service." He lowered his voice. "My belly, however, is my own."

"Sire, you know that bread from your kitchens is cake for the gods. If the court on Olympus feasts so well, surely that is why they are immortal. And look! It is just now out of the ovens, warm and fresh, begging to be eaten."

"I am a mortal yet I live like Demeter, goddess of the harvest, feasting on the product of her grain, blessed to serve a magnificent monarch. May your shadow never grow less!"

Ulysses whispered, "Only you can so easily turn a clear act of larceny into blatant flattery. Which do you enjoy more, eating the bread or stealing from the women?" Without waiting for a response, he leaned over.

"Stay close Bates! Within the next few days I will need your eyes and ears as never before." The twinkle in Eurybates' eyes vanished, and a strange firmness settled in.

"And by the way, ... break off half that loaf for me."

With mock dignity Eurybates twisted and tore the bread. He placed half in Ulysses' outstretched hand. The king headed for the palace entrance.

Passing through the main doors, he turned toward the workshops and storerooms built against the eastern wall of the compound. If Laertes was not away at his farm, he was most likely here. Approaching the sheds Ulysses heard workmen moving animals, sawing wood, amidst shouts and talking.

He entered a doorway, and a hammer banged against metal in an adjoining room. Ulysses heard his father grumbling.

"Bring me another piece of copper and try not to split this one!" Laertes roared to a servant. The old man glanced up, saw his son and immediately looked down at a wooden plow resting on a low worktable. Ulysses drew near, and his father mumbled, "Damned copper splits too easily when they bend it. Bronze is better."

"Father, Menelaus comes."

"I know. Heard it this morning. You were already gone." Laertes continued to inspect the plow.

"Would you like to share some fresh bread?"

Laertes looked up and met his son's gaze. Without a word the older man reached behind and grabbed a cloak hanging on the wall. He guided his son out of the workshop to a bench alongside the front of the shed.

Ulysses broke the bread and handed his father the crust. The young king outlined his thoughts, eyes staring at the ground. His father listened, nodded occasionally and munched on the loaf.

"Father, what do you think?"

"About what?"

"My logic. Is it solid? And is this eastern war as foolish as I think?"

"Your reasoning is as solid as the walls of Troy. No question about that. As for the foolishness of this war ..."

"All wars are stupid, Ulysses. That doesn't matter. Menelaus will chase his wife to the east, and he will drag all of Greece with him." He lifted his gaze to the sky. "What direction are we looking?"

"West."

"Son, our real opportunities lie to the west, not the east. I moved to these islands to escape the squabbling that consumes the Aegean. It's hard to get away from it. If a real challenge comes against us here, it will be from the west or from within. The east has plenty of its own problems."

"But your immediate concern is Menelaus. He is bright and noble although poor in his choice of women."

Laertes stood and looked at the sky. Ulysses rose with him. His father spoke softly, addressing the clouds. *"We look west, but we're pulled east."*

The older man patted his son on the shoulder and headed back to the shop.

# An Ancient Call to Arms

Two days passed before the ships appeared. They came at first light; five black boats heavily coated with tar and pitch. Each was manned by forty freemen and several nobles. There were twenty oars, every freeman alternating when his partner tired. The nobles gave the orders and guided each vessel.

The ships came to rest on the eastern side of Ithaca. Skimming close to shore, each boat lowered its sail and slowed. Dropping anchors in the shallow water, men poured over the side of each vessel.

At first sight of the ships sentries relayed the news by runner to the palace. Ulysses sat on his throne in the center of the great hall. Huddled around him were Laertes, Polites and Eurybates. The hunchback was talking.

"Five ships for one monarch? Maybe our Spartan king is confused over who stole Helen! Does he need two hundred men to convince you to honor your oath?"

Ulysses said, "It's about the right number, Bates. One or two boats would not be grand enough for the leader of this campaign. Many more than five would be too much to approach an ally."

Polites asked, "You think he will lead the force against Troy?"

"I doubt it," Ulysses said. "He's an able warrior, but no great leader."

"Maybe that's why he wants you so desperately." Eurybates ventured.

"No. He wants my brain, my sword and my men, but he won't ask me to lead. This is an Aegean war."

"Maybe Achilles?" suggested Polites.

Laertes said, "Achilles is a tremendous warrior, but he's a hothead. Agamemnon will lead. He is king of Mycenae, Menelaus' brother and a strong leader. He's the best choice. The Aegean empire revolves around Mycenae so he has the biggest interest in trade. Between the two of them they will unite most of the kings. It will take every one for a chance of success."

Ulysses was quiet for a moment. "When they come, stay sharp. Bates, you watch the king's entourage."

He turned to Laertes. "Father, are you ready?"

"Yes."

"All right, we wait. It shouldn't take them long to arrive."

The room warmed as the sun rose.

Noise erupted outside. Shuffling of heavy feet, strong voices. The door swung open and Eurybates entered.

"Great King of the Ionians, cunning warrior on whom the sun rises and sets, I present the lords of Sparta and Mycenae, Menelaus and Agamemnon."

They entered side by side. Ulysses recognized Menelaus from his visit to Sparta. Tall, blond and well built. They walked to within ten feet of the throne, which sat one step above the hall floor. Ulysses made no effort to rise.

Menelaus spoke. "King of Ithaca, I come as your ally and friend. I come with respect, bearing gifts to honor your virtue and stature. However I come with tragic news. Paris, bastard of Troy, has kidnapped my queen. I ask you to fulfill the blood-oath you swore to defend Helen with your life."

Ulysses was silent.

Menelaus glanced in his brother's direction. Agamemnon was taller, more solid, and his face bore the hard lines of a merciless man.

"Lord of Ithaca, this is my first time in your presence. I come as my brother's ally, by birth and in honor. Paris came as a guest to Sparta, negotiating for Troy. Befitting our sacred hospitality, my brother received him. The Trojan pig repaid our nobility with the foulest treachery. The divine Helen, whom we are all pledged to defend, was violently stolen. In fifteen days the kings of Greece gather at Egion. We unite to slaughter the Trojans and rescue the queen."

Ulysses remained silent. *Greek nobility, Trojan duplicity and the brotherhood of Greeks to rescue Helen. Nice argument. No mention of Trojan taxation of Mycenaean shipping or Helen's willingness to flee her husband.*

He rose and addressed the two men. "Good kings! You honor me with your presence, you have made a long journey and my heart is disgusted with this shameful act of cowardice. We are noble men. But, ... " Ulysses let his last word hang, "my oath is to *defend* your peerless queen not *rescue* her."

Agamemnon's eyes narrowed. Menelaus said, "She was taken by force, secretly, in violation of every decency ordained by the gods! You *must* honor your oath!"

Ulysses moved and stood in front of the two visitors. "Menelaus, you are my friend and a fellow king, but you forget yourself. You ask my help, and you are in *my court.*"

"King Ulysses," Agamemnon interjected, "this is a matter of your sacred word, a blood-oath you swore before the gods."

Ulysses glanced at the taller man. "Agamemnon, you are my guest here. Please make yourself comfortable in my home. There are rooms for you and your brother, and your men will find space in the guest quarters against the western wall. I will send supplies to the oarsmen on your ships. Tonight we dine here in the palace. You will enjoy our fine food and drink, and we will talk more."

Ulysses walked back to his throne and faced the visitors.

Agamemnon lifted his hand in farewell. There was no humor on his face. Menelaus mirrored his brother's gesture. They turned and were gone.

Ulysses looked at Laertes. "Well, Father?"

Laertes' eyes were on the door. "You played it well. You gave no ground."

# The Banquet

Ulysses spent the afternoon exercising with Polites in the *palaestra*, the wrestling compound beside the gymnasium. After the workout they took a short swim then sat on the beach, looking across the channel at the mountains of Cephalonia.

"Polites, what do you think of our two visitors?"

"Menelaus seems like a capable man, probably a good king and an able warrior. He yields to his brother, and Agamemnon makes the decisions. In battle I want Agamemnon on my side."

Ulysses gave a slight grunt and rose. "Let's rest before the banquet. We need to be sharp. We will eat little and drink less."

The two walked up the hill. Reaching the palace they gave each other a rubdown with olive oil. Ulysses relaxed as the oil worked its way into his skin. Afterwards he reclined for an hour, dozed lightly and awoke refreshed.

The setting sun rested on the mountains, bathing the palace in a rosy glow. Ulysses changed from his daytime tunic to a finer set of garments, drawn together at the waist by a wide belt woven with golden strands and held together by a large metal buckle studded with semi-precious stones. He heard the cooks move about on the floor beneath him.

Fully dressed, he walked to the window past the bed he had built around a giant olive tree that grew up from the first floor of the palace and through his bedroom. When the palace was constructed he left the tree in place and built around it. Then he thought about how to form the trunk as part of his marriage bed. He made it the bedpost, crafting it so it was impossible to move or dismantle the bed without destroying the room and that part of the palace. It represented the indestructible bonds of marriage.

Darkness fell. Ulysses walked down the steps heading for the *megaron*, the banquet hall beyond his throne room.

In the center of the *megaron* was an open hearth. The fire was low, giving off heat and sparkling light against the night. Near the wall beyond the fire were several wooden tables slightly larger than the ones that ringed the hearth. Four comfortable chairs covered with skins sat behind the larger tables. Stools were scattered about the hall. Eurybates appeared.

"Everything in order, Bates?"

"Sire, the room is set up; the food and drink are sufficient and on schedule; the entertainment is ready."

"Well done. We won't speak the rest of the night. Move away."

Eurybates was gone in the shadows. The king's eyes moved around the hall. Polites was nearby, speaking quietly with two young Cephalonians.

Noise rose at the entrance. Dressed in splendid robes Menelaus and Agamemnon entered, faces and hair shining with oil. Their men followed, eyes bright, sweeping the *megaron*. Walking across the room Ulysses stopped before the kings, spread his arms in a gesture of greeting then clasped Menelaus' hands.

"Greetings, my friend. It is good to see you at my fire. Perhaps tonight I will pay back a portion of the hospitality you showed in Sparta."

"I look forward to it."

He stepped between the brothers and guided them to the opposite side of the room. Ulysses indicated two of the fur-covered chairs for his guests. Polites, Eurybates and several locals moved to speak to the other strangers. The men spread in a loose circle around the hearth. Ulysses motioned to a servant who placed jars of wine and water on the tables, along with double-handled clay cups decorated with paintings of fish, dolphins and olive trees. Appetizers, *mezedes,* followed the drinks. Plates of octopus, squid, olives, bread and goat cheese. Soon the guests were laughing and sampling food, mixing the wine and water. Laertes entered wearing an elegant robe, salt and pepper beard well groomed. Ulysses and the two visitors rose.

Agamemnon said, "Laertes, it is our honor to be in your presence. Even in Mycenae your reputation is strong and admired. May your days be long and full."

Laertes' eyes rested on the tall king. "Agamemnon, you and your brother grace us with your visit. Your father was the most skilled man with horses I ever met. May we honor his memory tonight."

Ulysses placed a cup in Laertes' hand. Gazing directly at Agamemnon, the older man lifted the vessel just below eye level.

"To Atreus," he said. "May our horses serve us as well."

The three younger men imitated Laertes' gesture. Each sprinkled a few drops on the floor as an offering to the gods then took a small sip. Laertes took his place, and the others seated themselves. Slightly to the left, closest to the foreign kings Eurybates talked with several guests. He was in the midst of a dubious story about Cretan women. To the right and across the room Polites listened as another guest gestured and spoke. Agamemnon broke the silence.

"Your toast was kind, Sire. My father was a skilled breaker of horses and a strong man."

"It is said he had a sixth sense," Ulysses added, "that he knew the thoughts of the horses and communicated with them."

Agamemnon laughed. "Mycenaeans can be as stubborn as horses and as faithful in battle. As to whether much intelligent thought passes, - "

Ulysses rose. Without a word, he moved across the room toward several women entering the *megaron*. In the center of the group Agamemnon saw a tall, blond, average looking person. She surveyed the room until she saw Ulysses moving toward her. Her features softened, eyes brightened, and a very natural smile gave her a new face.

Agamemnon had seen many striking women. His wife, Clytemnestra, was beautiful. His brother's stolen wife, Helen, was dazzling. However there was something singular about this person. Before he could think further they were beside the table, the queen's arm locked in her husband's.

The men rose, and Ulysses said, "Agamemnon. Menelaus. May I introduce the queen of Ithaca, my bride, Penelope."

Menelaus kissed the back of her palm. "Good queen, you grace this land."

Penelope nodded and looked at Agamemnon who took her hand as his brother stepped back. "Queen Penelope, your husband has treated us as wandering gods in disguise. I had no idea he was married to a goddess."

Penelope said, "Good kings, you honor my husband and I with your presence. I hope you enjoy your visit and our hospitality. May you return to your homes safely with good ... *memories* of us."

Menelaus said, "Good queen, please honor us with your presence."

"Thank you, no. Tonight is for you men. You will have more freedom to speak without us."

Ulysses said, "Please excuse us for a moment." Penelope took her husband's arm and looked at Laertes for the first time. "Good night, *Patera-mu.*"

Laertes kissed her on both cheeks. "Good night, my daughter."

Penelope and Ulysses moved across the room stopping to speak to some of the guests. Sensing their mistress departing, her female escorts disengaged from their conversations. Reaching the door Ulysses kissed Penelope lightly on one cheek, and she was gone.

The night moved on. Bards took turns chanting poetry as each strummed a lyre, the five-stringed harp used to punctuate their melodies. They sang of gods and goddesses, distant lands, valiant men and noble women.

*****

Today the Greek bards remain. On any Sunday morning, at any Greek Orthodox Church in the world, you can enter and hear them. The Orthodox service is like no other, and the Greeks take great pride in how little it has changed. Much of the liturgy is recited from memory, delivered in melodic modulating tones by the priests and chanters. A sense of timelessness prevails, as you observe a worship service developed over the past seventeen hundred years, which grew from a culture much older.

The Orthodox service is a time machine. When today's priest begins to chant, he's transformed into an ancient poet educating his listeners. The spirit of Homer mingles with the spirit of God.

*****

More food arrived: roast lamb, vegetables and bread. When everyone was full to bursting, servants delivered grapes, figs and apples on wooden trays. One singer finished a song of brave men in far-off battle and Agamemnon spoke. "Ulysses, your bard sings of our coming campaign to Troy."

"He never mentioned Troy."

"My friend, in fifteen days we assemble. War is what we kings are made for. A glorious battle in a righteous cause. We rule with strength and we reap glory, capturing what is rightfully ours, the blood of less noble men dripping from our swords. Join us. It is your oath, your duty and your destiny!"

"Agamemnon, your cause is just. Your brother's wife was stolen. I am a Greek king, and my sympathies lie with you, but my kingdom is in the Ionian not the Aegean. I do not pay tribute to the Trojans. I have no merchant fleets traveling the seas. This *business* ... with Troy is not my concern. Your power is quite sufficient without me."

"No, you're wrong. Two men are indispensable in this campaign. Achilles ... and you! Achilles is the greatest warrior in the land. Without his strength we cannot succeed. We must have both his power in battle and the pride he gives the Greeks."

"*Ulysses, ... you are the most cunning leader in our world!* You're young, but your exploits on Crete and Delos are already legendary. Without your mind, eloquence and daring, ... we are doomed!"

Ulysses swallowed hard and spoke with difficulty. "Agamemnon, you honor me with your words. I will think on this." Abruptly he turned away.

To his left Eurybates reclined at a table with two Mycenaeans. A wild look passed over the young king's face. He squirmed in the chair, hands clenching and unclenching as he looked down, head moving from side to side. He rose, looked straight at Eurybates and roared, "Herald, come here!"

The servant looked into the crazed eyes and leaped to his feet, knocking over a stool and jarring cups on a small table. He scurried over to Ulysses. The king grew more agitated. "You pathetic hunchback! Bring us proper wine, this swill isn't fit for pigs!"

Eurybates raced in the direction of the kitchen. All eyes were on the frenzied king. Laertes rose and motioned toward Polites. Gently putting his arms around his raving son, Laertes spoke softly as Polites took Ulysses' other arm.

He calmed slightly and placed one hand on the side of his head. The two men led him toward the doorway, and Polites motioned to another man. They exchanged words then the other man and Laertes guided the young king from the room.

Polites returned to Menelaus and Agamemnon. "Good kings, I'm sorry my master left so quickly. I fear there was something wrong with his food or drink. I'm sure a good night's rest will revive him. Please relax and enjoy yourselves." Polites moved across the room.

Menelaus said, "I'm speechless. I don't know what to think."

Agamemnon sat and leaned back in the chair, fingers spread across his lips. "That was not bad food. Something else is going on."

"You think it's the *epilepsia?*"

"No, I've seen that before, more than once. This reminds me of grandfather when I was young, when you were still a baby."

"The madness?"

"Yes. There were unexplainable outbursts. Grandfather was fine for a while then an episode of screaming and running around. Finally he moved to a quiet part of the palace. I saw him very little after that."

Menelaus said, "Too much strong drink can cause fits of delirium, but I wouldn't suspect Ulysses of excess. Perhaps his extreme craftiness has unbalanced his mind."

"Perhaps."

Eurybates returned to the room with a jar of new wine. He looked around, moved to his table and spoke to the two Mycenaeans. "What happened? I heard they took Ulysses away."

The taller guest, Palamedes, quickly detailed what happened.

Eurybates looked toward the door and mumbled, "Again."

Palamedes reached for his shoulder. "You mean this has happened before?"

"Unfortunately, yes. There have been several incidents. They seem to be increasing, coming more often.

Eurybates looked around. "Please excuse me." He scrambled from the room.

Palamedes and his companion approached the visiting kings. Without waiting for a greeting Agamemnon said, "Gentlemen, please sit down. All at once, there are two very vacant seats at this table."

The smaller man, Alastor, spoke. "The herald says these outbursts have happened before."

No one responded. Agamemnon surveyed the room while the others talked. Neither Ulysses nor Laertes returned. The guests began to leave; the evening was breaking up. Agamemnon's people lingered in the hall waiting for he and Menelaus.

The older king stood and placed his cup on the table. "Palamedes! Alastor! Remain here after we leave. Keep your ears open, see if you can pick up anything of interest. We will talk tomorrow." He and his brother departed.

## First Light

Agamemnon tossed and turned all night, his mind troubled. Dawn was breaking when his half-slumber was interrupted. Muffled shouts and rapid footsteps bolted him upright. He threw aside the blanket and reached for his dagger. Grabbing his clothing in two steps he was at the door, clenched knife hovering near his hip.

The noises grew louder. He froze for a moment then flung open the door and slid into the hallway. *Empty!* It was three steps to his brother's room. He gave two distinct raps.

"Menelaus!"

The door opened instantly.

"What is it?"

Agamemnon raised a hand, eyes peering down the hallway. He glanced at Menelaus. "Are you ready?"

His brother disappeared into the room and returned fully clothed. They moved toward the palace entrance. Near the central door people rushed about, women's voices high-pitched and hysterical, men loud and agitated.

People streamed through the courtyard gate. Agamemnon looked right and saw his men running toward him, Palamedes and Alastor in the lead. The smaller man arrived first.

"What is it?" he said, catching his breath.

"I don't know." Agamemnon replied, moving toward the gate. "Come on!"

A dozen men formed around the kings as they pushed through the main opening. Just outside they froze.

Hurtling across the field in a one-man chariot was Ulysses, red hair streaming, eyes blazing. A powerful horse and a young bull pulled the chariot, bumping and struggling against one another. Fastened by long leather straps, a plow dragged and tumbled ten feet behind.

The men ran to the edge of the field. Agamemnon stopped and slowly sheathed his dagger.

The chariot thundered toward them, and Ulysses reined in his team, cutting a wide turn. The carriage aimed itself in the opposite direction, and Ulysses brought down a whip hard on the flanks of the bull. The animal reared, twisting its horned head and nearly gored the horse hitched alongside. The bull came down; Ulysses screamed and slapped both beasts with the reins. They picked up speed.

One of Menelaus' men swore softly. "King of the gods! Those two animals will kill each other yoked together like that!"

Screams and wailing rose behind them. Other men and women ran up. Among them were Penelope, Polites and Eurybates. Penelope clutched an infant to her breast.

Agamemnon's head jerked upward, mouth opening. He turned and spoke to his men. Menelaus moved back a step, a strange expression on his face.

Ulysses made another wide turn at the far end of the field. The horse reared, came down quickly and the team gathered speed, accelerating toward the onlookers.

Suddenly Agamemnon slapped Palamedes on the shoulder, and they moved toward Penelope. Palamedes wrenched the baby from the queen's arms. Penelope screamed and clutched for the child, but Agamemnon grabbed her from the rear. Menelaus and Alastor were behind Polites and Eurybates, relieving them of their daggers.

Palamedes raced across the open field holding the crying infant. He stopped in front of the oncoming chariot now only forty yards away. Hiding the baby until the last possible moment he spun around, lifted the child high then placed it on the ground in the path of the chariot. Palamedes moved to one side leaving the helpless infant facing the thundering hooves.

Ulysses pulled hard to the left and reined the team away from the baby. The animals reared as the chariot ground to a halt, the bull bellowing like it had been struck. Ulysses jumped down, ran to where his son lay, picked him up and stroked the crying baby's tiny head. The child ceased whimpering and snuggled close to his father.

Agamemnon released his grip on Penelope. Menelaus had moved onto the field alongside Palamedes who stood twenty feet from the Ithacan king. All eyes were on Ulysses.

The Spartan said softly, "Ulysses, … you are not mad."

Raising his head the Ithacan king looked at Menelaus then turned and gazed across the field at Agamemnon, still standing beside Penelope. The fire was gone from Ulysses' eyes. Breaking the silence he spoke loud enough for all to hear.

"Agamemnon of Mycenae, hear this! In fifteen days I will be at Egion with twelve ships and five hundred good men. We will surge across the Aegean Sea, smash the walls of Troy, slaughter the barbarians inside and rescue your brother's wife. In generations to come poets

will sing of two things. The greatness of Greek warriors
... and the burnt ashes of mighty Troy!"

Shifting his gaze to Palamedes, Ulysses walked
toward him until they were close enough to touch.

"Palamedes, know this! If my chariot had not
turned you would now lie dead on this field. I would
feed your organs to the vultures, and wild dogs would
tear apart your carcass."

Finally, looking straight at the Spartan king he said,
"Menelaus, take your men, ... *and get off my island!*"

Without another word he walked past them and
carried his son across the field to Penelope.

# Departure

Two weeks passed quickly.

Agamemnon and Menelaus would gather all the kings, convincing them to join the campaign. Lining up Ulysses' support first was a crucial part of their plan. Agamemnon's description of Ulysses' cunning was not empty flattery. Although still a young man he was considered ingenious, persuasive, diabolically tricky. He had nearly convinced Agamemnon of madness. It was a brilliant ruse, designed to sway a man who had grown up in a part of Greece where there were many rumors and stories of insanity.

The ships assembled, the prow of each boat painted the color of fresh blood. Ulysses watched the final preparations. Tomorrow they would sail. With the sun touching the western peaks, Ulysses walked up the hill for his last night on Ithaca.

He and Penelope ate quietly in a small room next to their sleeping chamber. Beside the dining table was a small cradle where Telemachus made soft noises. Ulysses leaned across the table and ran his finger across his wife's cheek. The sharp, sweet odor of gardenias drifted from the darkened balcony.

They finished and he walked to the terrace. Penelope carried the baby to the next room where his nurse waited. When she returned her husband was gazing east. Trailing a long tail of bright lights, the Great Bear was high in the northern sky. Orion the Hunter hung over the horizon in the direction of Troy, his slanted belt of three stars dangling a nebulous sword. Penelope came alongside her husband and placed an open hand in the middle of his back.

Hours later dawn broke gray and cloudless. Penelope rolled on her side and opened her eyes. Ulysses lay beside her, gazing at the bedpost formed by the olive tree. He leaned over, kissed her on the cheek and rose.

He dressed quickly and left the palace. In less than two hours the fleet would cast off. Each of the nobles had a history of loyalty, and every one brought the most trusted freemen he knew.

Polites and Eurybates were at the ships. Many of the crew were Cephalonians: fine warriors, able sailors but untrained navigators heading into unknown waters. They would hug the coastline.

Ulysses walked to Polites, busy supervising the loading of supplies. "Ready?"

"Soon."

The women, children and old ones gathered on shore. As the last men arrived and the remaining supplies were loaded, Polites walked to the lead ship where Ulysses and Eurybates inspected shields and swords. "All ready, Sire."

"All right," said Ulysses, "Say goodbye and cast off."

Most of the men walked to a woman on the beach. Some wives carried young children. Single men approached parents, brothers or sisters. Sobbing erupted, some of it muffled, some loud. Ulysses walked to his queen who stood beside Laertes. She held Telemachus in her arms.

"Goodbye, my treasure. I will return." Gently he took her face and kissed the lips. Looking down he cupped his hands around the baby's head and kissed the tiny eyes.

Turning to the older man Ulysses said, "Father, I will come home. I am the son of Laertes."

"You are the father of Telemachus."

Penelope handed the baby to its nurse and leaped into her husband's arms. They held one another for a long moment, then Ulysses pushed her to arm's length and let go. He turned and walked to the ship.

"Polites!" He shouted, leaping over the side onto the deck. "Cast off!" Raising his voice, "We go to slaughter Trojans!

A rolling roar rose from five hundred throats. Many men raised an arm, some with clenched fists, some with swords. They clamored toward the boats and pushed off, vessels gliding away from the beach, engaging oars.

Ulysses was at the front of the first boat, hand on the blood-red prow. As the sail fluttered up he looked straight into Penelope's eyes, lifting an arm in farewell. Turning, he gazed south at open water. A chorus of low moans rose from the beach.

Each sail blossomed in the wind, ships merging into a fleet. They gathered speed, and the oars were pulled in. Polites was at the tiller. Ulysses stood with his hand on Eurybates' shoulder.

The herald glanced at him. "Troy cannot stand against a united Greek army; we will be home quickly."

"Bates, let us take a sacred oath," he replied. "We may lie to our enemies. We must speak the truth to one another. We will be gone a long time."

The fleet neared the southern end of Cephalonia and in the distance lay the flowered island of Zakynthos. Looking straight at Polites a few feet away, Ulysses shouted, "Hard to port!"

Immediately the king spun around and looked halfway to the front where Eurybates anticipated the next command. Ulysses cupped his hands over his mouth and roared. "Bates! Trim the sail for port!"

The single sail was a huge rectangle hung from a large beam at the top of a central mast. The boat had been moving with the wind at its back, sail perpendicular to the line of the ship while the vessel surged south. Now Eurybates shifted the cable attached to the bottom left corner of the sail toward the front of the boat. Another sailor on the other side of the ship mirrored Eurybates' movement, moving the right hand cable toward the rear of the vessel.

The boat turned left and leaned hard right. Polites set the direction while Eurybates and his counterpart made small corrections in the angle of the sail making sure the vessel did not capsize.

The chance of one of these ships turning over was low. Ulysses' boats were short and squat, built for strength and stability not speed. Fast ships of renegade pirates did roam the seas, particularly the Aegean where rich merchant cargoes made tempting targets. The vessels of the buccaneers were long and sleek with extra sets of oars and larger sails. Some of the pirates fitted bronze-covered battering rams to the fronts of their ships, allowing them to smash the sides of a merchant boat just below water level. They would overpower the crew, loot the cargo then abandon the sinking trader. The marauders could generally outrun anyone who might pursue. For this reason Aegean cargo ships often traveled in groups for protection.

Pirates were the last thing on Ulysses' mind. None would come near a fleet of twelve ships full of five hundred fighting men. The king made his way up the left side of the vessel toward Eurybates. Drawing close, Ulysses shouted over the wind, "Not bad for a herald! Be careful, I don't want to play with the fishes!"

Eurybates grunted without looking up. He was a crafty chameleon. Eurybates could play the buffoon well, but underneath the foolish façade worked a sharp mind. Because of his posture and clowning demeanor many did not take the herald seriously. That was a mistake. In addition to a keen mind Eurybates was hard muscled and quick.

The boat headed toward the mainland. Out of the shelter of the islands the sea was rough, the wind gusty. Moving up the side of the rocking vessel Ulysses passed a nobleman standing by two seated oarsmen. The king leaned over, "All right, girls! Anyone who gets sick swims to Egion."

The waves and the hours streamed by. With the sun setting behind them, land emerged from the hazy horizon on each side of the boat. A pointed peninsula jutted out on the right. The wind lessened as the mainland to the north began to block it. The point of land grew larger, passed them on the right and the sea calmed. The lead vessel swung to starboard.

The ships drew close to shore, trees framing the beach. Ulysses ordered the sail loosened and it collapsed, the boat drifting to a near stop. Eurybates cast the anchor. The other vessels imitated the lead boat, and twelve black ships quietly bobbed near land.

Ulysses passed the word to wade ashore. They built fires on the beach, ate an evening meal then returned to the boats. Rather than camp on land the men slept on board near their weapons. Sentries were posted.

## Egion

Ulysses roused them at dawn. After a quick breakfast they cast off. The ships approached a narrow passage.

The Corinthian gulf is a small model of the Mediterranean Sea. They sailed through a Gibraltar-like strait, and the gulf widened on both sides to form a large oval-shaped body of water running west to east. At the far end was a narrow isthmus. The city of Corinth commanded the band of land that separated the gulf from the Aegean Sea. In the same way at the eastern end of the Mediterranean Sea a narrow isthmus separates it from the Arabian Gulf and the Indian Ocean. Many centuries after Ulysses canals were dug across both stretches of land. Today the Corinthian canal connects its gulf to the Aegean Sea. The Suez Canal links the eastern Mediterranean to the Indian Ocean.

The fleet sailed on. Large and arid like North Africa, the Peloponnesus lay to their right. This was southern Greece; it held the kingdoms of Argos, Mycenae and Sparta.

On Ulysses' left lay northern Greece. Like Europe on the north side of the Mediterranean it was green and mountainous, crowned by Delphi the geographical and spiritual center of the Greek world. Clinging to the side of a great mountain, the village of Delphi hovers over a deep ravine. The chasm spills into a verdant plain that flows like a smooth green river to the gulf. Legend says Zeus once released two eagles, one where the sun rose and another where it set. They flew toward the center of the earth and met at Delphi.

Mystic and still, this was the home of the ancient oracle. Speaking in strange riddles, the prophet foretold the future in puzzling ways.

Modern scientists discovered that seismic cracks running through Delphi emit gases with hallucinogenic properties. Women who served as spokespersons for the oracle in ancient times appeared in a trance-like state, the result of exposure to the drug-laden vapors.

The boats sailed into the morning sun. By midday Egion appeared, its docks filled with ships. Sails and prows with distinctive markings represented individual kingdoms. Ulysses moved his vessels beyond the harbor and anchored.

On the beach Ulysses gathered his two friends. "Polites, you remain here. Set up camp, then drill the men. There's no sense being idle. They will just get homesick, argue or drift into town and get into trouble. Eurybates and I will go to the meeting."

He looked toward the town. "I hope this gathering goes quickly without much squabbling. We're headed into conflict; the best way to meet it is head-on."

Eurybates asked, "You expect dissension?"

"With Greeks, always. These are proud men, and Agamemnon asks a great deal. Most of them see both profit and risk. They'll display their prominence and angle for as much influence as possible. This will be the first real test of Agamemnon's leadership. It is one thing to convince a single Ithacan king. It's quite another to unite the entire land in a difficult and dangerous struggle. We thirst for glory and a display of manhood, but we're not fools."

He glanced at Polites. "Any questions?"

No response. Turning, he said, "Let's go, Bates."

They started toward town just as a large chariot drove up. The driver pulled on the reins and ground to a halt. Ulysses recognized him as a Mycenaean who had accompanied Agamemnon to Ithaca.

"Good king! Your ally Agamemnon sends his greeting."

"Your king also sends this transportation?"

"Yes, Sire!"

They climbed in. The driver roused the horses and sped off.

Three days passed. Polites drilled the men, practicing with swords, shields and spears. They worked hard, ate well and slept soundly. Polites set the tone with a mix of sternness, encouragement and occasional light-heartedness. In the evenings he circulated among the campfires, laughed at stories and eased any dissent with a light word.

Just after sundown on the third day the chariot reappeared. All eyes watched as Ulysses and Eurybates climbed off.

Polites walked quickly to the approaching men. "What is the word?"

Eurybates replied. "Just as Ulysses feared, a bunch of damned arguing and strutting! I've seen better displays from roosters!"

"Well, do we head for Troy?"

Eurybates hesitated and looked toward his king. Ulysses was silent, his face placid. "We go my friend, but not to Troy. The fleet assembles at Aulis. We go to find Achilles."

Polites' eyes widened. "What do you mean? He wasn't here?"

"No. Agamemnon had difficulty convincing the kings to go against Troy without our greatest warrior, but at least he got a commitment from them to assemble the fleet."

"Where is Achilles?"

"There are all kinds of rumors, nothing certain. Agamemnon convinced the kings that I can discover his hiding place."

Eurybates cut in. "It was quite a feat of salesmanship. Agamemnon spent plenty of time persuading the crowd that Ulysses could not only find Achilles, – but also enlist him in the campaign."

"Where do we start?"

"Aegina," Ulysses replied, "Tell the men."

## Toward Aulis

The next morning the fleet moved east with a new mission, ... retrieve Achilles. Full of nervous energy, Ulysses moved back and forth across the boat. By mid-afternoon he was beside Polites at the tiller. Ulysses gazed across the gulf. Rising from the water a row of purple peaks spread across the northern horizon, crowned by a huge mountain like a giant throne in the center of the range.

Polites glanced at his friend. "It was long ago."

"You saved my life that day."

"You got the boar with the first thrust. He would have died quickly regardless."

"No. I was young and rash. Excited and proud to be hunting on Mount Parnassos with my grandfather and uncles. I rushed the boar when he burst from the thicket. It's true my first blow was good. I caught him right above the shoulder blade, and the spear went deep. But I was off-balance. He would have killed me if you hadn't distracted him."

"You're a great hunter, Polites. You understand the spirit of the animals. When I charged you moved with me like a shadow. You lunged and screamed just as I struck. The boar was distracted and instead of his tusk slicing me through the middle, he caught me on the upper leg."

"Ulysses, the spear is your first, best weapon. I've never seen anyone handle it like you. You're as powerful as many men a head taller. Those taller ones are usually clumsy. You handle the spear as well as most men handle a sword."

The king looked back toward the mountain. "You saved my life that day, ... and that boar will save my life at Troy."

"What do you mean?"

"That day I learned to manage my passions. Ever since I've tried to act without emotion. I was impulsive. I lost my focus, and it almost killed me. You caused the boar to lose his focus. That did kill him."

"Polites, when we go to war we kill Trojans one at a time, but we don't lose control of ourselves in battle. If we get caught up in the excitement of combat it could be fatal. When this is all over, you and I are coming home."

Ulysses turned toward his friend. "Why don't you get something to eat? I'll take the tiller for a while."

Polites moved toward sacks of food and wine propped against the side of the ship. The fleet sailed on. Toward the end of the day the richest city in Greece came into view.

Corinth had grown wealthy because of its position. The isthmus was a convenient spot to portage boats overland to the Aegean Sea. Ulysses' ships docked at the harbor, then gangs of slaves pulled the vessels from the water using strong cables. They dragged each flat-bottomed boat over a long series of logs. At the end of the four-mile crossing the ships were again slid into the water. This avoided the long and dangerous voyage of over three hundred miles around southern Greece.

Ulysses anchored the fleet on their first night in the Aegean. He could hardly have guessed that his vessels would remain in this sea for ten long years.

The next morning he called the men together. "Bates, you remain here with the other boats. The men have worked hard the last couple of days. Let them enjoy the pleasures of Corinth. Polites and I will take the lead ship and go to Aegina. Meet us in three days in the straits of Salamis."

Two nights later a lone vessel glided toward a wide beach on the east coast of the island of Aegina. Waves breaking on the sand shone in the moonlight. The boat ran aground, and men slipped over the sides. They gathered quickly.

"Eurylochus, take half the men. Leave some with the ship and post sentries near those trees," Ulysses said. "The rest of you come with me."

He moved inland with a dozen men. Their objective was the sacred grove of the local goddess Aphaia.

At this point in history Aegina was a prosperous island of merchant seamen. Its sailors roamed the Mediterranean and Black Seas. In the years ahead Aegina grew in prominence. Its ships ranged as far as Spain where the discovery of silver spurred Aegina to mint coins. Bearing the island's emblem, the Turtle Drachma became the first silver coin produced in Europe. At the main port on the opposite side of the island Ulysses had learned that the priests of Aphaia dealt in various rituals, some religious, some very practical. A few of the priests were links in a vast intelligence network, their information supplied by the mariners of Aegina.

Past the line of trees a cart path led to the interior of the island. Cicadas buzzed and fireflies flickered as they walked up a gentle rise. Polites leaned toward his friend. "Why Aegina? The oracle at Delphi is more prominent and highly regarded for information."

"Aegina is the ancestral homeland of Achilles. His father was one of three princes of the island. There was a family feud, the favorite prince was killed and Achilles' father fled. We're walking into the center of an information network. Many here are loyal to Achilles; a few are enemies. But one thing is a good bet. Someone, either friend or foe, will know his whereabouts."

"So you figure the priests are the best sources of information?"

"The best and the safest. We should avoid any squabbles with the *Myrmidons.*"

"*Myrmidons?* Ant people?"

"Aegina is named for a woman who bore a son to Zeus. That son became ruler of the island and the grandfather of Achilles. The wife of Zeus sent a plague on the island in anger over her husband's infidelity. Most of Aegina's people perished in the plague. The king then asked Zeus to repopulate the island with as many men as the ants he happened to see on an oak log. Zeus granted the wish. That is why the men are known as Myrmidons."

Polites looked sideways. "You believe that?"

"The truth is probably something less but close enough. Once we get Achilles committed to war these are the men he will lead into battle. Right now without their leader they're uncommitted, and that's another problem. Agamemnon desperately wants Achilles, but he also needs the warriors Achilles can bring together."

Thirty minutes walking brought them to a grove of cypress trees on a prominent hill. The sound of the sea faded, and a light breeze flowed across the grove.

In years to come a grand limestone temple dedicated to Aphaia emerged on this spot. The shrine changed its allegiance from one goddess to another depending on the fortunes of Aegina. Aphaia would yield first to Artemis, goddess of the hunt, and finally to

Athena as the nearby city-state of Athens grew powerful. Eventually, three of the finest monuments in Greece, the Parthenon in Athens, the temple of Poseidon at Cape Sounion and Aegina's temple rose in an equilateral triangle, each one approximately twenty-seven miles from the other two. The Greeks built brilliant structures on marvelous sites, their knowledge of architecture harmonizing with a keen sense of natural beauty.

Past a line of cypresses the men entered a clearing with two stone buildings. Several figures in white robes approached, their faces ghostly in the moonlight. The tallest one stared at Ulysses.

"What do you seek?"

"I search for wisdom and knowledge from the goddess of the grove. We have come far and need the guidance of the gods."

"The goddess Aphaia is our patroness. We also honor Artemis, goddess of the hunt. Which of the divines do you worship?"

"I honor Aphaia; my friend is devoted to Artemis."

The pale man said, "You come with me; your companion will go with him." He pointed to one of the other men.

Without a word the other attendant turned and led Polites toward a circular structure on the right. Nearing the building's entrance Polites saw two young women robed in light clothing. The escort motioned to the women and spoke to Polites. "The servants of Artemis will lead you in your quest." He slipped away.

A cool female voice confronted Polites. "What do you seek of the goddess?"

Polites looked into a clear, tanned face resting on an athletic frame clearly outlined beneath the fabric rippling across her body. This was not a person who spent her life shut up in a religious sanctuary, but one who ran in the fields and bathed in the sea. The energy of an active life simmered behind the respectable image of a temple priestess.

"I am a hunter, and I desire the blessing of the goddess in my efforts," he replied. "I also travel far, and I seek information for my journey."

"What kind of information?"

"I am a hunter of animals, but soon I will hunt men and they will hunt me. For success I must have the best hunters with me. Those I seek, and your goddess may help me find them."

"Follow me."

She led him into the building while her companion remained at the doorway. They entered a large room lit by blazing torches. In the center was an elevated platform holding a bronze altar. The odor of incense drifted about, and a man in dark robes stood at the altar, his back to them. Whispers of white smoke rose just beyond him. Polites and the young woman approached, and the priest turned. Short hair, a long beard, hands folded in front.

She spoke to Polites, torchlight gleaming in her dark blue eyes. "The priest of Artemis does not speak to worshipers. Tell me your request. I will convey it to him."

"I seek a great warrior, the descendent of gods. His father was a prince of Aegina, but the father was banished. The warrior is in hiding. I wish to know where."

"Wait."

She ascended the steps, approached the priest, and spoke softly and quickly. The priest mumbled a few words then the girl returned to Polites. "The information is available, but it comes at a high price. What are your intentions toward the warrior?"

"To enlist him as an ally."

"What do you offer?"

Polites reached into his robe and produced a heavy pouch. The priestess took the sack and carried it back to the priest. He accepted it without interest, and she retraced her steps to Polites.

"Follow me."

"Where do we go? I just paid a considerable price."

A smile hinted at the edges of her mouth. "The goddess is honorable."

She led him out of the building to a clump of trees on the edge of the clearing. They sat on a marble bench, and she was silent.

Polites said, "Will I receive what I need?"

"The priest would not accept your offering if there was no chance of success."

"What is your name?"

"Daphne."

"Aegina is your home?"

"Yes. My family has served the goddess for generations as priests and priestesses."

"It is a noble work."

"Some would not say so. Many laugh that the temple of Aphrodite uses its priestesses for love rituals."

Polites said, "I know that the sanctuary at Corinth engages in those rites. Does it go on here?"

"No. Artemis leads us in a cult of chastity. Each priestess remains a virgin as long as she serves the goddess. All the priests must marry, but they are forbidden to marry active priestesses."

"How long will you serve?"

"As long as my family and I believe I am valuable to the goddess."

They lapsed into silence, but Polites was strangely agitated. Comfortable with large numbers of rough men, this solitary female unnerved him.

Without warning she rose. "It is time."

They reentered the sanctuary. Daphne approached the priest who stood motionless at the altar. He spoke quickly without expression. After a few moments he turned his back, and Daphne rejoined Polites.

"The warrior you seek travels to the island of Skyros with his mother Thetis. There you will find him," she said. "Now you must go."

Once again she led Polites into the moonlight. At the entrance she turned. "I hope the services of the great goddess Artemis profit you."

"I'm sure they will." Polites looked across the clearing where the rest of the men stood in the shadows.

"Will you walk with me to the edge of the grove?"

"My place is here at the sanctuary."

"Your place is not here forever, and my place is not in battle. Walk with me; I am trustworthy."

Daphne hesitated only a moment then they moved toward the entrance of the clearing. She said, "You say your place is not in battle yet you go to a great conflict. Why?"

"I serve a king. He is my monarch and my friend. I hold his life in my hands."

They neared the entrance of the grove. The men from the ship stood nearby.

Polites turned to the priestess. "Daphne, when this war is over I will return to this place, and I will ask if you must still serve the goddess."

She smiled broadly. "You are a lonely man living with warriors, and your passions carry you away. Perhaps you have little experience with women, and before you lies danger. I am one woman and my purpose is here."

"I don't believe that. You were raised in a family, and family is your destiny just as it is mine. I have known women, but none whom I will share my life with. You speak with confidence, you laugh with honesty, you serve with honor and you are led by principle, not passion. I suspect you love the forests and the sea as I do. You are also beautiful. I will return, and I will offer you the same allegiance I give to my king."

Polites allowed himself a smile. "However I expect a different relationship with you."

She looked surprised but not startled. He reached toward her, grasped one of her hands and kissed it. Without giving her a chance to respond he walked toward the men.

Daphne lingered in the moonlight, staring at him. He looked back as he neared the group. Silently she lifted her hand, then turned and walked back to the building.

Polites watched until she was out of sight. The men began to tease him and make lewd comments. He did not respond. Footsteps came from the shadows, and Ulysses appeared with a questioning look. "Any luck?"

"Skyros."

"You're sure?"

"Yes. How about you? What did you find?"

"Nothing, but it doesn't matter. We have what we need. Let's go!"

In the morning they joined the other ships nearby in the straits between the island of Salamis and the mainland. Here in a later time a united Greek fleet using startling tactics swamped a huge Persian armada. The men of Aegina made a large contribution to that victory.

Turning east they sailed past the small city-state of Athens. In millennia to come it grew into the greatest city in Greece, dwarfing all others. The fleet sailed on hugging the coast, following the Attic peninsula to Cape Sounion, the most easterly tip of the mainland.

The boats rounded the cape and headed north, wind now in their faces. The sail on the lead vessel came down, and Ulysses shouted to engage oars. The men began to row in unison, starting their chant slowly, increasing cadence until a comfortable pace was set.

The other ships mirrored the leader's movements. Their sails fluttered like wings of gulls just landing on water. They engaged oars and inched up the coast, swimming into a bay-like entrance formed by the mainland and the island of Evia.

They passed an area destined for fame in years to come. The site of a historic battle. The name of that coastal plain thunders down through history, a symbol of cunning heroism … *Marathon!*

Here the Greeks defeated a superior Persian force with a novel strategy. As the armies faced one another across an open field, the Greek commander placed his weakest force in the center to concede where the Persian army was strongest. The Persians attacked and the middle of the Greek army retreated. Their strong forces on the left and right swung and attacked the invaders on the wings, sandwiching the opposing force. The enemy was routed.

Mindful that the Persians intended to attack Athens from the sea at the same time as the Marathon battle, the Greek commander sent a runner to carry the victory news to the city twenty-six miles away. Then he rallied his exhausted troops and began a forced march back to the capital. Meanwhile his courier ran the distance, delivered the victory message, collapsed and died. Two thousand five hundred years later, today's twenty-six mile marathon is the classic, international long distance race.

Past Marathon the channel narrowed. Ulysses' ships passed a tiny village named Graea, an example of how small things can change history.

The land of Ulysses, Achilles, Helen and Menelaus is properly known as Hellas. The Hellenes are the principal race that the people of Greece consider their ancestors. To the present day this country, culture and people describe themselves and their world with these terms. Foreigners use the words "Greece" and "Greek" to describe Hellas and the Hellenes.

In the centuries after Ulysses the Hellenes spread throughout the Mediterranean world, building colonies and spreading their culture. The people of Graea established a settlement in Sicily, and the local people used the term "Graek" to refer to these new colonizers and all the other Hellenes. The term "Graek" stuck fast.

The Hellenes accepted the description reluctantly, in the same way they have always reacted to outside description, pressure or domination. To this day when you arrive in Greece you do not hear and seldom see these "foreign" terms used. The country is *"(H)Elatha,"* the people are *"(H)Elines,"* the language *"(H)Elinika."*

Aulis sat on the coast. Immediately to the east and parallel to the mainland Evia was the second largest of the Greek islands. In generations to come Evia's capital Chalkis grew into what Mediterranean cities can be, a harmonious mix of Christians, Moslems and Jews. Now this area was the rallying point to rescue the woman whose face would launch a thousand ships. The channel between the island and the mainland provided a large, calm harbor to organize for the campaign.

The ships of the armada gathered like sea-borne ants, each working independently yet united with a common spirit and temperament only they could understand.

Ulysses signaled his fleet to anchor at Aulis. The flagship continued a short distance to Chalkis, situated on a narrow strait where Evia almost touched the mainland.

Drawing stares from people on the pier, the black ship eased into the harbor. Polites and Eurybates guided them to a vacant area and threw lines that men on the dock grabbed.

The harbor was a bustling series of inns, taverns and places to buy supplies and equipment. Ulysses said, "We need a navigator who can get us to Skyros."

Eurybates replied, "There should be plenty around here."

"The man I want must not only get us to Skyros. He must know these waters well enough to take us to Troy. No sense doubling back, the fleet might already be moving. Besides, once we get Achilles, moving straight to

Troy will whet his appetite. There'll be no holding him back."

Polites said, "I haven't understood this business. Achilles is the greatest warrior in our land. There is no question about his strength, skill or courage. Some say he's invincible. His blood should be boiling for war. Why the reluctance? Why the hiding?"

Ulysses looked at the wooden planks beneath his feet. "Polites, the oracle has prophesied that *Achilles will die at Troy!* His mother has hidden him on Skyros. She doesn't want to sacrifice her only son for any reason."

Eurybates moved between the other two. "Well men," he said, licking his lips, "that *taverna* looks like an excellent place to find a navigator!" He guided them straight toward the building.

An hour later they emerged without a seaman but with valuable information. Over the past twenty years the city of Chalkis had built a colony on the island of Skiathos, off the northeastern tip of Evia. Skiathos was part of the Sporades, a group of islands sprinkled in the north-central Aegean. Skyros lay to the southeast of the Sporades cluster. The men of Skiathos knew this area better than anyone else.

Ulysses looked north. "Well, it's decided. We go to Skiathos."

## Skiathos

The next day the twelve ships moved up the channel. They reached the northern edge of Evia and turned toward open sea. Ulysses glanced to his left where a series of high mountains butted against the water. On those peaks in years to come a small band of Greek warriors held off a huge Persian army. Their heroic stand became a legend.

At a mountain pass called Thermopylae, seven thousand Greeks blocked a Persian army numbering in the hundreds of thousands for two long days. On the third day the Greek commander learned his force had been betrayed and circled. He dismissed all but three hundred of his own men, elite Spartan warriors. Fighting to the death before the crushing Persian advance, they bought precious time for their comrades to escape.

The ships entered the Aegean and Skiathos lay before them. Low and wooded, a floating oasis on a sparkling sea. The island grew larger; a long stretch of golden beach faced the fleet. Signaling to the other boats, Ulysses aimed his flagship toward land and ran the boat aground on the soft, yellow sand. The other vessels came to a halt alongside the main boat, and the captains of each ship gathered on the beach around Ulysses.

"We'll be here a few days," he said. "Have the men make camp. Tell them to enjoy themselves this evening in town. It could be their last taste of Greek life for quite a while."

Looking at Polites and Eurybates he said, "Let's go. We need to do our work and find our man before the town is overrun by Ithacans." The three of them headed toward the main settlement.

"This is wonderful!" Eurybates said, eyes roving up and down the hills. "I didn't know Aegean islands could have so many trees. Reminds me of home."

Ulysses said, "Remember we're looking for a man who can do the job. Someone we can trust. Or at least someone who is dependable if paid!"

They walked east and climbed a small rise. As they crested the hill the island's main port appeared below them. A series of buildings around a sheltered, circular harbor fringed with pine trees. A tiny islet floated offshore.

Moving down the slope they passed small homes with noisy children, screaming mothers and squawking chickens. At the waterfront a small squat building held a sign over the door displaying a crescent shape and the words, 'Pale Moon.'

They entered a dimly lit room with long, low tables. Men with the look of the sea stopped talking and surveyed the three strangers. Ulysses whispered, "Bates, you circulate. See if you can find any likely candidates. Polites and I will take a seat."

All three moved to a high table at the rear of the room where a man was cooking. Ulysses ordered a plate of fried fish, a loaf and a jar of wine. He paid with a small lump of silver, then he and Polites took a table against the wall. As Eurybates moved around gesturing and joking, the faces of the local men softened.

Ulysses broke the bread, and Polites poured wine into two cups. He mixed it with water from a jar already on the table. Gently touching the vessels together Polites said, "May our way be strong, swift and successful!"

"So be it, with the strength of the gods." Ulysses replied.

Each took a sip, munched the bread and looked around the room. Some of the weather-beaten men were missing fingers. Those with canes jerked their arms and heads as they spoke.

Eurybates approached, accompanied by a short wiry-looking man with the face of an old hawk. Beak-like nose, squinty eyes and hollow cheeks.

Eurybates addressed Ulysses. "My friend," careful not to use his king's name, "this man claims he knows the way to Skyros."

Ulysses glanced sideways, "You have a name, old man?"

The hawk's eyes sparkled. "Son of the gods, I am Nereus. I was born on the Aegean and know these waters better than my own name. I can guide you to Skyros. Salt-water courses through my veins, stars dance in my mind and sea currents flow through my heart. I have the eye of an eagle and the sense of a dolphin. If you need someone to guide you to Skyros, I am your man!"

"You talk well," Ulysses replied. "Sit down!"

He grabbed a stool. No one offered him food or drink. After a moment Ulysses said, "Curious that you hold the name of a sea-god. Did you make that up?"

"No, my lord. My father was a Phoenician trader. My mother is from Skopelos, between here and Skyros. She gave me the name to honor my father's sailing skills."

Polites rose, motioned to Eurybates and they moved a few steps away. "Go check out his story."

Ulysses turned and faced the stranger. "Do you know Skyros?"

"Of course, sire. Like the back of my salt-crusted hand."

Ulysses leaned over and dropped his voice. "Describe it to me. And know this! I have twelve ships and five hundred warriors anchored at the golden beach over the hill. I would slit the throat of any of my men who tried to trick me, and I certainly won't hesitate to carve you to pieces."

The islander's face went blank, but his eyes did not retreat. "I speak smoothly, but I do not lie. And certainly," he paused, "not to a king."

"Go ahead then."

"Skyros is a strange remote island, larger than Skiathos. The fortress of Lykomedes lies on the east side facing the winds. There is a small harbor there but the water is rough. The better harbor is on the west coast. The palace of the king is a high citadel. The main access is through a cave-like passage up the side of the hill. Makes the fortress easy to defend."

"The north end of the island is wooded and lush, similar to Skiathos. Most of the farming goes on there. The southern end is completely different. Barren and dry like the Cyclades with a tall mountain in the center. It's an island of fine horses; the Skyriots are able riders."

"How do we get there?"

"The Sporades are sprinkled like pebbles across this part of the Aegean. Sailing them is like walking on rocks across a great lake. You must only know where the stones lie. Skiathos is first, then Skopelos, and in a direct line beyond, Skyros. A few small islets lie in between. Uninhabited, but good landmarks. We follow the line of islands with the east coast of Evia on our right."

"You said the west coast harbor was better?"

"Yes, particularly with the size of your fleet. You mentioned twelve ships. Linaria is on the calm side of the island sheltered from the open sea and the prevailing winds."

Nereus asked. "Are you an ally of Lykomedes?"

Ulysses reached for the jar of wine and a cup, pouring some liquid for the sailor. "No, but I am not an enemy."

Nereus continued. "I have never seen King Lykomedes. He is said to be a large man, tall but not heavy. They also say he can be brutal and merciless, but not without reason." The sailor lifted the cup to his lips.

"I need a man to get my fleet to Skyros," Ulysses said, "then I need someone to guide us toward the Black Sea."

The small eyes widened. "Then the rumors are true. You go to Troy."

Ulysses nodded and took another sip.

## On Skyros

Nearly sunset, the island of Skyros loomed ahead, gaunt and austere. Ulysses guided his ship into the harbor on the west coast while the remainder of the fleet anchored offshore. Although the dockworkers appeared to ignore the visitors, Ulysses was sure that news of their arrival had already reached Lykomedes.

A few years earlier the deposed king of Athens, Theseus, had retreated to Skyros under the sanctuary of King Lykomedes. The Athenian later died under mysterious circumstances. The story was that one evening Lykomedes took him for a stroll around the fortress, high above the harbor. At a strategic spot Lykomedes pushed Theseus over the cliff. The Athenian plummeted to his death on the rocks below.

Ulysses disembarked with eight men, and Eurybates went ahead to inquire about transportation. The king directed Nereus to stay with the ship. He gave instructions to a trusted aide to watch the navigator closely.

Eurybates returned. He had lined up several chariots for travel to the fortress. Ulysses led his men to the waiting carriages and they sped toward the citadel. Moving through a narrow valley, the sea disappeared behind them. Tree-covered hills hemmed them in on both sides; the setting sun shone on their backs.

The Skyriot horses were well built with muscular shoulders and legs, thick necks and finely shaped heads. They moved nimbly over the uneven terrain.

The sea reappeared ahead, and the hills on the right fell into the water. The road turned north with mountains on one side, pounding surf on the other. Coastal winds hit the men's faces.

They sped into a flat area. Against the sea jutted a lone, rocky crag. From a distance it looked barren and deserted. Drawing close, Ulysses saw buildings nestled in a depression against the landward side of the rock. A pirate or enemy approaching by ship could not see the settlement. Even now, knowing that Lykomedes' fortress perched on the *acropolis*, Ulysses saw no sign of life atop the peak.

The chariots halted at the base of the hill. Several stern men in palace clothing approached. The tallest man in the center of the group spoke.

"What is your business here?"

Polites stepped forward. "I am Ulysses, king of Ithaca. I come in peace to pay homage to King Lykomedes. I have further words for your king ... private words!"

The Skyriot looked back and forth at the nine visitors. "Follow me!"

The guards led them between the buildings and up the hill. After a few minutes they reached the entrance to a cave. The tall man turned to Polites. "You may come with me. Leave your weapon. Your men will remain here."

Polites looked at him evenly. "My men come with me and so does my weapon. Nine men are no threat to King Lykomedes in his own fortress. I come in peace, and I ask your king's hospitality as a fellow monarch."

The guard surveyed Polites. "As you wish." He turned and entered the cave. They followed into the darkness.

The passage was little more than head high, wide enough for two men walking beside one another. At intervals of ten feet flaming torches hung on the walls, lighting the way. After fifty yards the cave-like passage ended, and they walked into open air. The night sky sparkled. Ahead was a massive structure encased in natural outcroppings of rock. Mostly stone, partly wood. A huge door barred their way.

The guard rapped on the entrance, and it swung open. The men stepped inside, and the door slammed shut behind them. *Inside the lair of Lykomedes!*

The guards led them down a short, wide passageway and came to a set of double doors where more armed men stood. Their escort spoke a few words to the guards, and the Ithacans were ushered into a great hall. The *megaron* was a cleverly adapted cave, its ceiling high and uneven. On the far side of this rock-lined hall on an elevated throne sat Lykomedes.

He was a powerful-looking man, and his presence dominated the room. Beside him was a handsome woman nearly as tall. On either side of the monarchs were other severe looking men and several young women. A herald stepped forward and announced, "Great King Lykomedes, I present the lord of Ithaca … Ulysses."

Polites took one step toward the throne. The king's eyes were those of a wild bull, boring down on Polites. A booming voice echoed across the cavern. "Well, good king! What brings you to my home?"

Polites met his gaze. "I come to pay homage, King Lykomedes. We sail to Troy to reclaim Helen, queen of Sparta. She was kidnapped by the Trojans."

Lykomedes' lips tightened. "And what does that have to do with me?"

"I carry a message from Agamemnon, king of Mycenae, commander of the Greek armada. The message is private, but I know he wishes your help in this noble campaign."

Lykomedes laughed. "Ulysses, I bear you no ill will. But don't use the word 'noble' to describe either this misguided adventure or Menelaus' queen."

Polites raised his voice a notch. "I never used the word 'noble' to describe Helen."

"Very well. You and your men are welcome. Please join us for the feast tonight. We have good food, fine wine and wonderful entertainment. It is my honor to host you."

His gaze passed from Polites and swept the group. Lykomedes hesitated when he noticed Eurylochus, tallest and most handsome of the men. His gaze stopped again as he noticed Ulysses' physique. Lykomedes rose, approached Polites and extended his arm. "Please join my table. We would love to hear of your lands in the Ionian Sea. Your men may find places. They will be served."

Polites turned and signaled the Ithacans to make themselves at home. He motioned for Eurylochus to accompany him. They moved with Lykomedes across the room to a large table. Gentle music began. Other members of the court relaxed into private conversations; servants circulated with trays of food and drink. Ulysses grabbed Eurybates' arm, guiding him into the shadows away from the main party.

Ulysses asked softly, "What do you think, Bates?"

Eurybates' eyes swept the room. "He bought it! He has no reason to distrust Polites. He doesn't miss much, and I wouldn't trust him at all. He looks like the type who would stab his - "

"You think he knows why we're here?"

"If Achilles is here and Lykomedes knows it, then he realizes precisely why we're here. What do you think?"

Ulysses eyes moved around the hall. "I believe Achilles is here. I can feel it. It's the ideal hiding place. A remote island with an independent and cutthroat king. Lykomedes has no allegiance to the Greek cause. He mocks it. This place is perfect. If Achilles is here the king knows just where he is. His eyes and ears are everywhere. Let's circulate."

They moved in opposite directions. Across the room Polites and Eurylochus engaged Lykomedes, his queen and several men in discussion. Ulysses watched the young girls near the royal party. The queen rose, then the men stood, bidding her farewell. Ulysses looked for Eurybates who always had one eye on his business and the other on his king. He motioned and immediately the herald was at his side. Ulysses leaned over and said a few words.

They strode toward the departing queen as she headed for the main doors with two tall young women.

Eurybates spoke as they approached. "Good and gracious queen, we wish to thank you and your fine husband for your excellent hospitality. This will be our last memory of Greece before we go to Troy."

The queen stopped and nodded. Eurybates went on. "Your companions are like goddesses. Well suited for your heavenly presence."

A cold smile hardened her lips. "Are all Ithacans such shameless flatterers?"

"Goodness no, fair queen! I am one of a kind, but an oracle proclaimed at my birth that I would always speak the truth. This is the curse on my life!"

The queen's mouth curved into a wry grin. "My daughters, this is the kind of trickster it would be good for you to avoid."

Ulysses said, "Good queen, do you have sons as noble as these fine daughters?"

"We have five daughters."

"In that case you and your husband are fortunate, blessed by the gods. Sons are overrated compared to beautiful daughters. *And many Greek sons will die at Troy!*"

One of the girls went pale. The other one stared at Ulysses.

The queen said, "Obviously the death of foolish young men at Troy is no concern of mine."

Ulysses' eyes were unyielding. "Madam, it is our custom to give gifts to our friends and hosts. My king has a few tokens for your fine daughters. May we call tomorrow to repay your hospitality?"

"Of course. At noon. My reception area adjoins the *megaron.*" Turning, she announced, "We must go, ladies. It is unseemly to linger much longer in this room of men." The three of them walked to the doors and departed.

Without taking his eyes off the vanishing women Ulysses asked, "Bates, what is the king doing?"

The herald adjusted his tunic and glanced toward Lykomedes. Looking down at the floor Eurybates replied, "He's watching us."

Ulysses spoke toward the wall, away from the direction of the king. "Move away. We'll talk later." Eurybates strolled to a nearby group of men. Ulysses moved toward the shadows at the edge of the room.

The remainder of the evening passed without incident. The food was excellent and the wine less sweet than Ionian varieties. The bards were different, their dialect and melodies unusual. At the end of the night's festivities several of Lykomedes' attendants showed the Ithacans to a series of small rooms on the edge of the fortress. The cells were sparse, the beds simple.

When the attendants departed the visitors settled for sleep. Ulysses and Eurybates shared one room. Within a short time their door swung open, and Polites slipped inside. Ulysses sat on the edge of one of the cots, Eurybates on a stool beside him. Polites took the other seat.

"You first, Polites," Ulysses said. "What did you learn?"

"The king is one cagey customer. He gives away nothing and constantly probes for information. His questioning is skillful, sometimes blunt, sometimes ingratiating. He's relentless."

"Do you think he's suspicious?"

"Oh, he knows we're after Achilles. No doubt about it. However we were never alone and he never asked directly. I have a private audience tomorrow. I'm sure he'll get straight to business then. All in all, tonight he played the good host."

"No invitations for a midnight stroll along the cliff?"

"I said he was a *good* host!"

"What about the queen?" Ulysses asked.

"What about her?"

"Your impressions."

"Quiet and real smart. Knows everything that is going on."

Ulysses countered. "How about the two daughters?"

"Like the mother but a little more animated. Youthful energy, I guess. The one who is a bit fuller in the face seemed very pleasant. What I would call a rosy disposition."

Ulysses seemed to mull something over in his mind. After a moment he looked at Eurybates. "Well, Bates. How about you?"

"I've said everything I can about the king. I agree with Polites about the queen. She's a shrewd one, a good match for Lykomedes. I moved around and probed some of the locals. They're a close-mouthed, serious bunch."

Eurybates looked at Ulysses. "What was your purpose with the queen and her daughters? And why the appointment tomorrow? You could have avoided that."

Ulysses said, "I believe Achilles is here. I think that Lykomedes knows where. And I believe that the queen knows almost everything the king knows. That is why I went after her. I didn't want to go near him. Polites can learn just as much as I could and besides, Lykomedes might discover our deception. The queen is the best key."

"Why the questions about sons? You know Lykomedes has only daughters."

Ulysses looked at Polites. "Remember that rosy glow you noticed on the one daughter? She's rosy all right. *She's pregnant!*"

The jaws of both men dropped. "Well good doctor, how do you know that?" Eurybates asked.

Ulysses stared straight ahead. "Those two monarchs are both on the thin side. Large, powerful, ... but lean. So is the one daughter. She fits the pattern. The other one is full in the cheeks and has that glow that comes to happy, pregnant women with little morning sickness. Some can only gain weight when they're expecting. I suspect she's one of those. Her clothes were even looser than is fashionable for royalty. But I watched her while she sat, when she walked and as she turned. She is more than a little pregnant. She's starting to show."

Polites protested. "Lykomedes would never tolerate it. The girl is unmarried. There is no word of a husband or even an engagement. Lykomedes would kill any man who did that, and he might even kill his own daughter for being so stupid."

Eurybates added, "He's right. The girl is happy and pleased. If she really was with child she'd be dead or secluded and thinking about suicide, and the poor fool who got her pregnant would be at the bottom of the cliff."

"You're right. Lykomedes is a real butcher, no doubt about it," Ulysses replied. "He would kill ... *almost any man* ... who got his daughter pregnant."

Polites and Eurybates looked at each other, then back at their king. Eurybates said, "You don't think..."

"I sure do! Achilles is here. Lykomedes and his queen know it. Their daughter is unmarried and pregnant. She's happy about it, and even her parents are pleased. Otherwise she wouldn't be out circulating like a virgin."

"Something like this doesn't just make Lykomedes' day. It makes his whole life! How would you like to be a king like him with no son for an heir, yet possibly get a grandson who's the offspring of the greatest warrior in Greek history? Lykomedes is ecstatic!"

Eurybates leaned back on his stool and looked up at the ceiling. "So that's why you asked about sons, knowing full well she didn't have any."

"That's right. I wanted to see her reaction. More importantly I wanted to see her daughter's reaction. And I saw what I expected. The girl practically fainted when I talked about Greeks dying in the Trojan campaign. Remember, ... *Achilles has been prophesized to die at Troy!*"

The next morning dawned bright and clear. Ulysses had slept well. Right after they awoke he and Eurybates headed out of the fortress. They emerged from the cavern entrance, and the cluster of whitewashed buildings spread beneath them.

Reaching the bottom of the hill the king turned. "Bates, go to the ship and bring the sack we talked about. I'll be here in town when you return. Be as quick as you can."

Eurybates nodded and walked toward a group of chariots bunched on the road. Merchants were setting up booths in an open area off to the right. Ulysses moved toward the makeshift market.

Eurybates was back within two hours, carrying a large bag. He found the king quickly. "Do you have everything?" Ulysses asked.

"Everything you said. Did you get what you needed at the market?"

"Yes, let's get back to the fortress."

"What did you find out in town?"

"Rumors about Achilles are everywhere. No one admitted seeing him. If he has been spotted, few would be foolish enough to say so since he is under Lykomedes' protection. But the rumors are enough. There is so much talk it basically confirms he is here."

"So we proceed as planned?"

"Precisely."

They entered the fortress, passed several sober-looking guards and walked straight to their quarters. Once inside the room Ulysses took the sack, placed it on the cot and dumped out the contents. They surveyed the items, ensuring everything was there. Just before noon they left the room and headed down the corridor toward the queen's reception area. At the entrance two large guards blocked their way. Eurybates recognized one from the previous evening. "Hello my friend! We have an appointment with your fair queen."

The guard looked at the sack Ulysses carried on his shoulder then motioned toward it. "What's in the bag?"

"Gifts for your elegant queen and her matchless daughters!" Eurybates replied. "We repay grand hospitality, and you treated us like gods last night!"

"Open it up!"

"Certainly, certainly!"

Eurybates took the sack and set it on the floor. The guard placed his hand inside, withdrew it after a moment and barked, "All right. We have to check you for weapons. None are permitted in the reception hall."

"A wise policy, my friend!" Eurybates responded, handing the bag back to Ulysses. "We are unarmed."

The guards moved in front of the two Ithacans, spread open their cloaks and assured of no hidden daggers, stepped back. The main guard said, "You may go in. The queen is expecting you."

They walked through the entrance into a bright, well-decorated room with a long table in the center. At the far end sat the queen with several young women. A few of the girls wore veils. Stone carvings and silken tapestries lined the walls in contrast to the otherwise barren character of the fortress. Some of the women were taller than Ulysses. There were close to a dozen present.

Eurybates walked to the head of the table. "Good queen, the light of day shows your nobility and beauty in much more accurate detail." He spread his arms. "Which of these ravishing beauties are your daughters?"

"I was correct last night," the queen replied. "You are a shameless flatterer. Don't think I am taken in by empty words."

She looked down the table and motioned for some of the young ladies to approach. Five young women without veils stepped forward. Ulysses judged them to range from around fourteen to twenty years in age. The rosy-cheeked girl from last night came forward first.

The queen said, "This is my oldest, Deidemeia."

She looked at the two Ithacans cautiously and nodded.

"And these are my other daughters, ... Pasithea, Eurynome, Danae, and Charis."

Eurybates intoned, "All noble names for beautiful young women." He surveyed the five females. "May your lives be long and contented, your husbands blessed by the gods. May your children give you honor."

Ulysses watched Deidemeia.

The queen looked at Eurybates and her eyes narrowed. "I expected your king to accompany his gifts."

"He sends his regrets, madam. He has an audience with your husband. So the delightful and honorable task of presenting these items falls to my companion and I. So if it pleases you, noble queen, may I?" He gestured at the table.

"Certainly."

With a flourish Eurybates motioned for the sack. The young women gathered around Ulysses as he placed it in the center of the table. The queen remained seated, and Eurybates continued to babble. "Of course my queen, these gifts are mere trifles to bestow on creatures as exquisite as your fine daughters. But we do our best to show our immense gratitude!"

Ulysses opened the top of the bag and quickly spread the items. The girls gasped and murmured as a series of fine necklaces, bracelets, rings and earrings sparkled before them. The jewelry was both gold and silver, with intricate filigree work and dazzling semi-precious stones inlaid on many of the pieces. The last items to fall out were two jewel-encrusted daggers. They looked out of place with the other ornaments.

The girls examined the pieces, draping bracelets and necklaces around their wrists and necks. Deidemeia stood near her mother at the head of the table.

Ulysses grabbed the two daggers and tossed one to the far end of the table. Unsheathing the other weapon, he threw the cover aside and moved toward Deidemeia. He raised the knife to strike.

Her eyes and mouth sprang open. She stepped back, screamed, and a loud shout came from the opposite end of the table.

"Drop that knife Ithacan, or you won't draw another breath!" One of the women held the other dagger. She ripped off her veil and revealed the enraged face of … *a man!*

Ulysses dropped his weapon on the table and said, "Achilles, I am Ulysses, lord of Ithaca. I would never harm either this woman or her unborn child. I am here to ask *you* to join us in glory on the fields of Troy!"

Silence hung in the room. The doors burst open and guards rushed in, swords drawn. Without looking at the armed men Achilles lifted his other hand and commanded, "Hold fast!"

They froze. Achilles grabbed the collar of the woman's robe he wore and in one movement ripped it from his body like it was paper. Underneath he was dressed in simple peasant clothing. He was as broad and well built as Ulysses and as tall as Agamemnon. A tiny smile spread across his lips as his right hand relaxed its grip on the dagger.

"Well done, Ulysses! I've heard of your cunning," he said, "Now I know."

Achilles shifted the dagger, raised it above his head and in a mighty downward sweep drove it into the table. Nearly the entire blade sank in solid wood. The table shuddered.

In many ways Achilles was a typical Greek son. Although the entire Trojan War came to revolve around this splendid warrior here he was, clothed like a girl and hidden among the king's daughters to avoid a fight. The reason? - Mother said so.

It was a brilliant strategy. Who would think to search for a brutal fighter in the pampered company of the royal princesses? It was like hiding a fox among the chickens.

Ulysses said, "Achilles! Agamemnon of Mycenae commands the mightiest armada in the history of the world. The lords of Greece sail one thousand ships against Troy. We will burn that decadent city to the ground. The kings know that without Achilles we cannot destroy Troy. With you we will slaughter the Trojans, and our names will ring with immortality. We will be like the gods! Join us!"

The rage on Achilles' face faded, and a new fire glowed and built in his eyes. The Ithacan plunged on.

"Achilles, every real king, prince and warrior in our glorious land sails with Agamemnon. Our sons and grandsons will hear the poets sing of the courage and might of their fathers forever. And chief among those men of valor will be the god-like Achilles, the greatest warrior in the history of the Greek world."

Lowering his voice to a whisper, Ulysses' eyes bored into the fighter's heart. "We are mortals, Achilles. This battle will make us immortal. Above all men Agamemnon wants you and I. Come with us! We will smash the walls of the mightiest city in the world. Our swords will drip with the rich blood of kings. Their treasure and their women will be ours. They will die. We will live forever!"

"Achilles, we are made for war. We have no other destiny. We have only this choice. Eternal glory on the fields of Troy ... or ... *oblivion in Hell!*"

The greatest warrior of his time looked into the eyes of the finest orator he had ever heard. Achilles' face was radiant. Ulysses knew he had won.

He walked the length of the table to where Ulysses stood beside Deidemeia and the queen. Glancing at the woman who carried his child, he looked at the young king and thrust out his arm. Ulysses grabbed it and they held each other firm.

"I will gather my men."

The stage was set for the most enduring battle in the history of the ancient world.

# *Troy*

Amidst great excitement Achilles' ships joined Ulysses' vessels on Skyros. Now in early morning darkness the dual fleet neared the coast of Asia Minor.

Dim light outlined a large shadow of land ahead. A murmuring buzz rose from the men as they strained to see what the horizon held. A mountainous coastline crystallized.

The giant Greek fleet overflowed the bay at the foot of the mountains. The sun burst over the peaks, and a cascading cheer came from Ulysses' ships. The first morning rays spread and pointed down like the arms of a bowing actor on a grand stage, gesturing to a huge audience of black ships stretching across the horizon.

It was hard for even steel-hearted Ulysses to remain unmoved. But as his men laughed and roared, Ulysses' mind focused on the heady words he used to snare Achilles. The Ithacan was under no illusions. Men talk proudly and nobly about battles and wars. When the fighting is an image in their minds it is romantic and exhilarating. The reality is not.

Wars are beastly affairs. People who wage war create victims, and they themselves are victimized. The Trojan War was no exception. When it was over there were no real winners. Those who survived carried deep scars, both physical and psychological, for the rest of their lives. Those who were dead ... were dead.

In the end the city of Troy was burnt to ashes, its men slaughtered, its women and children hauled off as slaves. Ironically the ten-year campaign began the decline of the Mycenaean trade empire. The best men of a generation deserted homes and kingdoms to fight a misguided war. While they were gone weaker, less noble men took their places. In addition a race of blond giants, the Dorians, pushed down from the north into this power vacuum. The victors had sown the seeds of their own demise. Ancient Greece entered its Dark Age.

The *Iliad* is the story of that war. The focus of the conflict was Helen; the combat centered on Achilles. He was a magnificent warrior, and his passions were his undoing.

In his introduction to Fagles' translation of the *Iliad,* Bernard Knox notes that Helen and Achilles were the two god-like characters in this drama. They were both willful and capricious, and they showed little concern for the consequences of their actions. They were like gods, and they were like children. Helen abandoned her family and ran off with a foreign prince, resulting in the death and suffering of countless men in a questionable war. While Achilles argued and pouted in the Greek camp, his best friend replaced him and died in battle.

Today this self-centeredness is as central to Greek character as it was in the courts of Olympus or the battlefield of Troy. Every Greek is like a god. Each acts autonomously with a lack of self-awareness that is amusing and powerful.

The people of Greece are a gang of mischievous children. They attack life with an innocence and self-absorption that is refreshingly alive. They are oblivious to the consequences of their actions upon others and self-contained in their initiative. The Greeks are great fun.

Although the Trojan War centered on Helen and Achilles the real, understated and ultimate hero of the conflict was Ulysses. Over and over he helped pull it all together. Ulysses constantly mediated with the quarreling Greeks, using all his powers of logic and eloquence to sustain the war effort. When it was appropriate he was a valiant warrior.

At one point Agamemnon was wounded and withdrew from battle. Hector, the Trojan champion, sensed vulnerability and hurled his forces at the enemy. Ulysses realized the tide had turned; the Greeks were in danger of being routed. He called on an ally and the two led a valiant charge, wading into the Trojan advance, cutting down warrior after warrior. An arrow hit his partner in the leg, and Ulysses stepped between him and the advancing enemy, giving his friend a chance to retreat. The other Greeks had fled.

Ulysses was alone. Troubled but calm he considered his only two options. Stay and face the Trojans alone or retreat. He quickly made his decision. Only cowards retreat in battle.

The enemy circled him, and his mind swept back to the boyhood image of he and Polites on Mount Parnassos, facing the great boar. He remembered his own words.

"Polites, you saved my life that day, ... *and that boar will save my life at Troy!* When we go to war we kill Trojans one at a time, but we don't lose control of ourselves on the battlefield. If we get caught up in the excitement of combat we will lose our focus, ... *and it could be fatal!*"

The reply of Polites came to him in a flash.

"Ulysses, ... *the spear is your first, best weapon!*"

Cornered like the boar, he watched the enemy close in. Suddenly Ulysses sprang toward the closest Trojan, coming down with his spear into the man's shoulder.

Ulysses cut down four more warriors one by one. The last one killed was brother to a huge man named Socus who saw his sibling fall. Enraged, he thrust his spear. It hit Ulysses' shield with such force that it drove through the shield and metal corselet, piercing the Ithacan in the ribs.

Blood oozed from the wound, but Ulysses controlled his emotions, fighting fear, remembering the boar. The wound was not fatal, but the blood was flowing. Within a few minutes he would weaken. He looked straight at Socus and his voice came like deadly ice.

"You're a dead man. You have injured me, but this is the last day of your life. Killed by my spear, you give glory to me, and your life to *Hell!*"

Socus turned to run, and Ulysses drove his spear between the Trojan's shoulders, killing him instantly. The corpse collapsed in the dust. Ulysses reached down, grabbed the other spear where it had entered his own ribcage and withdrew it. Blood spurted from the wound.

His enemies sensed a kill. They moved in. Ulysses stepped back, shouting for help. When one of the enemy moved too close, his spear shot out. His reputation was well known, and they had just seen mighty Socus fall.

Menelaus and the great Ajax were less than fifty yards away. They heard Ulysses' shouts and quickly understood how serious things were. The Ithacan would never call for help unless he was desperate. Menelaus turned to Ajax.

"That's Ulysses! He must be in trouble. We've got to help. If we lose him, it would be a disaster!"

They raced up a small hill in the direction of the shouting. Ulysses felt his legs losing strength, but he gave no sign of weakness. He kept his voice strong, lashing out. But his grip weakened. He grew light-headed.

Suddenly Ajax was in front of Ulysses, his massive shield coming down like a wall before the advancing warriors. Menelaus grabbed the Ithacan under the arms. They hobbled back toward their army. A chariot came over the hill, and Menelaus loaded the wounded king aboard.

Ulysses not only knew how to fight. He knew how to play. When the warrior Patroclus died in battle, the Greeks feasted and competed in games at his funeral. The third event was a wrestling match, first prize a beautiful cauldron worth twelve oxen. Achilles called for the contestants to rise.

Huge Ajax, the man who had helped save Ulysses on the battlefield rose along with the Ithacan king. Ajax was a head taller, and often in wrestling matches the taller opponent has an advantage.

They stepped to the middle, gripped one another and each tried to twist his adversary to the ground. Locked together, they circled and shifted, sweat and frustration building. Neither was able to gain advantage.

The crowd grew bored. Ajax whispered, "Ulysses, either let me lift you or you lift me, and let's leave it up to the gods."

Ajax moved to raise his partner, but Ulysses clipped him behind the knee, and they went down in a pile of arms, legs and dust. Struggling on the ground, again neither was able to gain advantage, and neither one would concede.

Achilles intervened and declared both men winners. The next event was the sprint, and again Achilles called for the contestants to stand. First prize was a massive, finely-crafted silver mixing bowl, the most beautiful of its type in existence. Although weary from his bout with Ajax, Ulysses came forward with two other swift runners.

The sprinters lined up; the race began. Ulysses allowed the younger, faster man to go ahead but stayed right on his heels. The Ithacan hung close to the leader matching him step for step, breathing down his neck. The crowd screamed for Ulysses to win and cheered him on. The runners neared the finish line ready for a final burst of speed, but the younger man stumbled and Ulysses surged past, winning the prize.

Ulysses confronted any fellow king when he sensed unwise thinking or action. He challenged Agamemnon, Achilles, anyone who stood in the way of victory. He coaxed, prodded and bullied his fellow Greeks. Whatever worked. At one point he grabbed an obnoxious soldier causing dissension and publicly beat him up.

When Ulysses spoke, his words drove home like an overpowering blizzard. His logic was uncontestable. Focusing on the task at hand, unclouded by personal passion he rallied his men. When Agamemnon or Achilles talked they were full of themselves. When Ulysses spoke, he was consumed by a desire to win.

After ten long years the war ended. His mission was over. Now there was only one thought in the mind of Ulysses, … *return to Ithaca!*

# Northern Greece

War weary and anxious to get home Ulysses departed Troy with his fleet. Many of his friends had fallen during the conflict. Eurybates and Polites were alive, but they were changed men. Quiet now. The joy they once felt in each other's presence was gone.

If anything, the bond between them was deeper, more serious. Ten years of savage struggle side by side made them even more like brothers. There was nothing they didn't know about one another now. Some things they wished they didn't know.

Ulysses planned to reach the shores of northern Greece. Then he would follow the coastline as it swung in a great southwestern arc toward Skiathos. From there he would retrace his steps to Ithaca. For years he had thought about little except how to defeat the Trojans. Now he would return and set his kingdom in order. Although he didn't expect the war to be short, he never dreamed it would last so long. What would he find at home? Were his mother and father still alive? Was his wife well? What of the infant son he left behind, now ten years old?

Ulysses looked at his men. They were agitated beasts. Ten years of living without the effects of wives and families had made them crude and coarse. On their way to Troy they were excited, animated and playful. Eager to squash those they called Trojan savages. Now Ulysses' men were the barbarians.

The fleet moved north. At the end of a day land appeared. A green coastline beckoned, the area known today as northern Greece, east of current day Thessalonica. His men were restless. Ten years of war had conditioned them to constant aggression. Night fell and Ulysses drew his ships into a small circular bay. He gave orders to pitch tents on the beach. They waded ashore, made camp and slept.

The next morning came with a cloudless sky. Ulysses rose and prepared breakfast. The men were full of nervous energy. Eurylochus approached.

"Sire, the men want to spy out the land. The people who live here are allies of the Trojans. We want the spoils of victory. It is our right. Lead us!"

Ulysses looked up. Eurylochus was like a god. The tallest and most handsome of all the men, a brilliant fighter. Countless times over the past ten years he had sacrificed and taken grave chances. Ulysses stood and strapped on his sword. "Gather the men."

Eurylochus ran back to his tent. Soon a noisy mob formed. Ulysses told Eurybates and Polites to stay in camp with any who didn't go.

They moved inland and devastated the countryside. Plundering goods, pillaging, stealing women. Three days later they straggled back to the beach and collapsed. Many slept for a day.

The reprisal came at dawn. A human avalanche of incensed natives rolled down on the beach. Some of the Ithacans had fallen asleep on the edge of camp, either too drunk or too exhausted to crawl into their tents. The peasants hacked them to pieces where they lay.

With the first cries of agony Ulysses was on his feet, grabbing his sword. Inside his tent he knew immediately what was happening. Screaming to Polites and Eurybates he ran outside and looked toward the hills, his first instinct to rally his warriors. His men were battle-hard soldiers. Tough, skilled and merciless. They could cut the untrained natives to pieces.

Instantly he realized that was foolish. They were outnumbered and his men lay in groggy heaps. Too many would die if they tried to fight. Raising his sword he screamed, "To the ships! Now! To the ships!"

Eurybates and Polites sprang the moment Ulysses shouted, hustling men and supplies toward the waiting boats. Most of the raiding party staggered to their feet, searching for weapons as the attackers descended. Ulysses waded into groups of his men, kicking and shoving, shouting his command again and again. Some struggled toward the water. Others were being butchered.

He lunged into the swarming natives, cutting down peasants easily and quickly, sometimes killing two with one powerful swing. It wasn't enough. He sensed the attackers overwhelming his men and at the last moment, he turned and raced through the water. Polites reached down and hauled him aboard. The oarsmen had the ship moving toward open sea.

Ulysses forced his way to the rear of the boat and looked back. All his ships were moving, men struggling aboard in the shallow sea. Luckily not many natives pursued them into the water. The locals seemed content to wreak havoc among the injured and dead on the beach. Ulysses took inventory in his head estimating how many had fallen. He guessed they had lost over seventy men.

He shut his eyes, turned away from the bloody beach and slumped to the deck.

## The Storm

The fleet limped out of northern Greece. Poseidon was the great god of the sea. During the war he was the ally of the Greeks. Now he turned his back on them.

A thick fog and violent wind burst from the north and drove the ships across the center of the Aegean Sea. The crew was terrified. Barely escaped from the wrath of the natives on the beach the men held on for their lives, ships buffeted and tossed southward. Scattered islands whizzed by, but the crew could neither see land nor did they care.

After a day of howling winds and rain, two islands appeared close together. The boats surged through the gap, and land partly blocked the raging wind at their backs. Ulysses veered hard to starboard, knowing the coast of Greece lay in that direction. Finally he had the courage to raise a sail, and the other ships followed his lead. The boats roared westward, leaning over hard to port.

Ulysses ordered the sail let out all the way to spill the wind. Even so, the tiny vessels were flung with new vengeance as the gale again gathered strength. The sound of sails tearing pierced the storm, and too late Ulysses screamed to lower them. Realizing his ships were in danger of being cast south out of Greek waters, he shouted to engage oars. "Row, men! Or tonight, we dine with Poseidon in Hell! Row, in the name of the gods! Row!"

His men bent to the task and for six hours they labored. Completely exhausted, many hoped for death and release from terror. At last Ulysses noticed the waves slacken although the wind continued unabated. He sensed land.

The men were mindless beasts. They rowed, unaware if their oars cut the water.

"Take the tiller, Polites!" Ulysses shouted. He stumbled and waded to the bow past men still rowing, switching off with those who bailed water as it poured in over the edge. He strained to see through the murkiness, wind slapping his face.

A shadow formed in the gray fog. A mountainous wall loomed, accelerating toward the boat. Ulysses spun around. "Hard port, Polites! Hard port!"

Straining for hours to fight his way to starboard Polites thought he heard wrong. Then he saw the dark cliff and swung the tiller. The wall of land skidded by. Again they entered fog with no hint of land.

Polites wondered if Ulysses had fatally erred. *What if we're swallowed by this merciless sea after being so close to land?*

The wind now came in fits and gusts. Polites felt like a boxer at the end of a match: without strength, beaten senseless, but relieved his opponent was also near exhaustion. For an hour they drifted.

The fog dissipated, and light entered the small world of their boat. Ulysses glanced back. A few men were missing, probably swept overboard. Another dark image formed ahead. Too discouraged to give an order to crewmen who couldn't carry it out, he gave up and watched the land close in on his vessel and scoop it like a giant ladle thrust under them. The ship ground to a stop.

He rolled over the side, collapsed on the sand and surrendered to unconsciousness.

# On Spetses

Twelve hours passed without Ulysses' body moving. A dreamless coma engulfed him. At midday faint sounds of waves lapping and wood creaking from the rocking boat seeped into his mind. The squawks of sea gulls broke his sleep. Ulysses tried to move, and sharp pain forced him awake.

His body ached; his head was splitting. His throat was a dry, twisted rope. Sensing the shadow of the boat, he rolled toward it and felt shade pass over his face. Ulysses lifted his eyelids, and light burned his eyes. Forcing himself upright he checked his body for injury.

Miraculously all the ships had survived, strung along the beach like wounded sea birds.

Ulysses spent the next two days checking the boats, making repairs to sails and resting. The island was Spetses: low, pleasant and wooded.

He understood clearly where they were, the southeastern edge of mainland Greece. The wind still blew, but less strongly.

There were two choices. Row against the wind north to Corinth and cross the isthmus to the gulf, returning home the same way they had come ten years ago. Or sail south and west around the Peloponnesus to reach Ithaca. His men were shaken and uncertain. The storm had beaten them badly, but the skies were now clear. Ulysses decided to sail around southern Greece rather than force exhausted men to row north against an evil wind. It was a fateful decision.

On the third day he launched the fleet south.

# The Odyssey:
## North Africa, Italy, and Beyond

The boats reached Cape Malea, the extreme southern point of mainland Greece, and the isle of Kithera lay ahead. They passed the island, the sky blackened and another storm descended. The wind and waves rose, and once again these warriors, so able in battle, found themselves helpless before Poseidon's fury.

Ulysses gave the order to lower sails and engage oars, hoping to hang near the coast. It was no use. For ten long days his fleet was hurled far to the southwest across foreign seas.

There are many theories about the actual route of the Odyssey. Homer's fantastic description allows great range for both his imagination and that of his readers. One of the most realistic plots of that voyage is laid out by Ernle Bradford in *Ulysses Found*. Bradford's account is written with the keen eye and practicality of a person who has studied the Greek world and spent a lifetime sailing the Mediterranean.

Ulysses and his men held on, and the tempest drove them over six hundred miles. They washed up on the shore of an unknown land, North Africa. Lost and disoriented, Ulysses wandered another ten years. Virtually the entire journey took place outside Greek waters.

Ulysses knew the storm had driven them far south. How far west was not clear. He headed north searching for home. The ships landed on the coast of Sicily. There a giant trapped and killed several of his best men. Ulysses outwitted the huge man, got him drunk with honeyed wine, blinded him and escaped. They continued north.

He searched for familiar coastline. The boats drifted west, skirting the island of Sardinia. Further north they sailed into a tall, natural harbor on the southern tip of Corsica. The natives attacked and Ulysses lost all ships but his own. Badly shaken, he and the one remaining crew headed east in a single vessel, realizing that Greece must be in that direction. Now the long peninsula of Italy blocked their path. He worked his way down the coast looking for a break in the land to continue east.

The further they traveled, the more men were lost, and the more dangerous the journey became. His sailors tired of the search. They did stupid things, but he needed them to get home. They lingered a year on the island of a beautiful woman named Circe. Her young maidens made his men forget their homes. Finally Ulysses shook them loose, and they continued down the coast. He and his crew passed through the straits of Messina between the island of Sicily and the toe of the Italian boot. At last he saw clear sea in the direction of Greece. Ulysses waited for favorable weather and launched into open waters.

Once again a storm struck the vessel and drove it south. The much-battered boat finally broke apart. Adrift in raging waters Ulysses lashed the mast and keel together. Clinging to what was left of his ship, several days later he washed up on the island of Malta ... alone. The world's first castaway.

He was truly marooned. Malta was a desert island. Barren, rocky with numerous caves, it received little rainfall. Sufficient water for some crops to feed the natives, but not enough for significant forests. The climate was comfortable. Even in mid-summer heat the sea winds made life pleasant. Winters saw no frost.

Ten years of brutal, bickering warfare had tested his physical and mental strength to the limit. Three more years of violent storms and wandering through unknown seas sapped him emotionally. He had lost every vestige of who he was. All his ships were sunk, his men missing. Everything was gone except the memory of home and his own life. Far from war, freed from the frustration of fighting to return home, his struggles ceased.

Malta was the island of Calypso, a ravishing woman with mystical powers who wanted Ulysses for her mate. He gave up. For the first time in his life he stopped striving. The man who had never known defeat was finally beaten. One year went by, then two, ... then five.

He wanted to forget. Ulysses sat by the sea, unfeeling, spirit dying.

He neared fifty years of age. A time when life should be settled. He should be on Ithaca watching a strong son prepare to take over the kingdom. Instead he didn't even know if his son and wife were alive. If they were alive, did his kingdom still stand? Or were Penelope and Telemachus slaves of some foreign king who devoured Ithaca as the Greeks had destroyed Troy?

The island of Calypso meant oblivion. He was alive, he was comfortable, but he was losing himself. His heart ached.

The modern Greeks are like Ulysses. They can't shake the memory of home. Many have emigrated to the United States, Canada, or Australia. The memory of who they are and the home they left is indelible. The land draws them like a siren's song.

Those who remain in Greece live in a society where home, family and land are part of their souls. Nowhere else can they experience that singular zest for life. The striking vitality of neighbors and friends with a rich, oral tradition built on a vast, melodic language. The indestructible family bonds forged by a long history of defending a home from the onslaught of invaders. The rampant individualism spawned by contentious, competing city-states.

Finally tears flowed down the face of Ulysses, the first sign his spirit still lived. He sat on the shore and wept. Large salty drops rolled down his cheeks, falling into the waves at his feet. Day after day he looked toward Ithaca. One day at sunset he rose.

His heart calm, he walked to the cave where he lived with Calypso and told her he must return or die trying. Survival was not enough. Ulysses had heard rumors of a forest somewhere on the island. He would build a vessel.

Calypso's eyes moistened. This man had been with her for seven years. Reluctantly she told him that on the far end of the island a hidden valley caught and funneled the moist trade winds. Only at the bottom of this ravine did large trees grow. Ulysses built a raft and rigged a makeshift sail. Using the prevailing west winds he launched his craft into an unknown sea. Without rowers if the winds failed, he would certainly perish.

He sailed for twenty days. On his left in the night sky was the Great Bear. On his right, Orion the Hunter. Using the Bear as a guide he sailed northeast. At last he sensed land ahead. Night fell.

One final violent storm descended. The raft broke apart. Clothed in a heavy fur he plunged into the sea. The waterlogged garment pulled him under. Struggling to stay afloat he stripped off the clothing and swam for the coast. The sea hurled him against a rugged shore, and he clung to the first rock. The surf wrenched him loose, tearing skin from his hands. The next waves battered him from behind and threw him on an open stretch of sand.

Naked and exhausted, he had no idea where he was. For twenty years away from home few strangers had helped him. Most had either tried to kill him, trap him or use him. He heard gushing water ahead. Half crawling, half-walking, he found a fresh water stream. Collapsing headfirst in the shallow river he drank in huge gulps, the water stinging his salt-lined throat. As he swallowed, the pain eased away.

He crawled from the river and walked upstream toward a rising hill, body convulsing from the chill. Bushes, then small trees appeared on each side of the river. Wary of wild animals that could attack, he scanned the underbrush.

A small dark gap appeared in the bushes, just enough for his body to slide through. He worked his way in, alert for any hint of a predator. Dry leaves filled a small depression behind the opening. He pulled his body inside, collapsed in the circular spot, covered himself with leaves and slept.

# On Corfu

*"Somewhere between Calabria and Corfu, the blue really begins."* Lawrence Durrell, *Prospero's Cell.*

Halfway through the next day Ulysses awoke with a start. He froze, senses alert. From somewhere down the hill came soft feminine voices. He strained to hear clearly.

Something was different ... *very different!* He looked up through an opening in the branches. The sky was a deep, rich blue he hadn't seen in years. The sunshine filtered through. It was soft and brilliant like liquid drops of gold, falling on his body and warming it. Sharp pungent scents glided on clear, dry air. The voices were soft and happy, and he could make out words. *Greek!*

Strength surged through him. He burst through the brush, looked down the hill and saw young women splashing in the stream. Some washed clothes. Others laughed and played with a ball.

Aware he was naked he grabbed some branches, covered himself as best he could and ran toward the girls. They looked up, startled by the movement and noise. Screaming, they ran toward their carriages.

One young woman stood beside the stream, looking at him strangely. Unclothed, his hair and beard were long bunches matted together, crusted with salt and sand. The magnificent body, still strong and powerful, was bruised and battered from last night's pounding. He stopped.

The girl was light-skinned and blonde. He slowed and walked to within twenty feet, not daring to go any closer. He looked straight into her eyes, opened his mouth and used his greatest skill.

Ulysses began a long, masterful poem, composing as he went along. He praised the beauty of the young girl. Without a break he candidly related his recent voyage from Malta, touching on the misfortunes he had suffered. In the end, he begged her help, finishing with a noble blessing and hope for her future.

The woman was stunned. Who was this strange creature? He had the body and presence of a god. Yet he stood before her naked and dirty, covered with sand and salt. She felt she heard an ancient poem but knew his words were only for her. She was drawn to him, and she was not one who liked being captive.

"Excessive monologues" like the speech of Ulysses to this young woman fill the *Iliad* and the *Odyssey*. When these prolonged discussions jump from the printed page and flow through real people, it's so Greek. So full of life. And you can still watch and hear it happen at any moment.

Wander through Greece today, and from the humblest village to the streets of Athens you see modern Homeric characters talking endlessly to friends and acquaintances. Given a chance Greeks jump on their personal stage, rambling on and on until their companions forcefully intervene in the conversation. Undaunted and unoffended by interruption, they catch their breath and launch into another speech.

He finished speaking, releasing her from his voice. She felt a huge presence had vanished. Yet he stood before her, shining eyes begging for help. Her heart leaped out to him. *This tragic creature needed her help!*

The young woman Ulysses addressed was Nausicaa. Her parents were rulers of this island, and like them Nausicaa was no fool. She knew this was a special person even though his appearance was horrid.

"Stranger, the gods treat mortals any way they wish. My father is king of this land. As a beggar who has suffered, you will be given clothing and whatever else you need."

Turning, she called her handmaids who had fled. "Take him to a place where he can bathe. Give him clothing. I will wait here."

She walked toward the carts. The servants led Ulysses to a bend in the river where trees and bushes grew thickly. A few girls ran back to the carriages, gathering oil and clothing for the stranger. When they reached the secluded spot Ulysses said, "Go and wait for me at your carts. It isn't proper for young women to remain here."

He scrubbed his body clean of sand and crusted salt. When his skin was free of filth and his hair smoothed out, he worked the olive oil into his skin and beard. Soon Ulysses glistened in the sunlight. He dressed in the tunic and cloak the girls left for him. Emerging from the trees, he walked toward the band of girls.

A few minutes ago he had been a huge, ugly animal. Now he strode toward them, head erect, hair and beard luxurious. Nausicaa spoke quickly to her girlfriends.

"Listen! Without help this man could never have survived. Before he looked like a beggar, now he seems like a god. This is the kind of man I want for a husband. Bring him something to eat."

Ulysses ate without a word. When he finished Nausicaa led him to her parents' city and palace. King Alcinous and Queen Arete reigned on Corfu, the greenest and most elegant island in Greece. He entered alone, went before the rulers, and beseeched their aid.

The *Iliad* and the *Odyssey* mainly describe action between men. However, the descriptions of Greek women are striking. Nausicaa was confronted on the beach by a huge, naked, barbaric-looking man. She stood her ground and directed the stranger to ask her mother for help, stating that if the queen agreed, this guaranteed his success. The hero obeyed.

Perhaps even more remarkable was Arete. It is apparent that she and Alcinous were *joint* rulers of Corfu. Recognizing the clothing that her daughter had given the Ithacan, it was the queen who first interrogated Ulysses, demanding that he explain how he came into possession of the garments.

King Alcinous and his fellow chieftains listened to Arete and responded to her directives. The king and queen were perceptive and wise rulers whose rich generosity to the stranger is mirrored in present day Greek society. They took Ulysses in and showered him with respect. After listening to his tale, they loaded him with gifts and delivered him by ship back to Ithaca.

The people of ancient Corfu were mariners whose swift ships were unmatched. Their city had massive walls, two excellent harbors, and delightful public squares. The palace was grand and tall, full of light with friezes carved in sky-blue stone. The thresholds were bronze, the doorposts silver and the doors themselves were fine gold. Inside the palace cloth of excellent design adorned the thrones.

The orchards burst with fruit said to grow constantly, summer and winter. The monarchs seated Ulysses on a chair covered with silver studs. He dined and drank their honeyed wine. Finally the king asked him to tell his story.

It is sad to watch Ulysses at this point. His long life of suffering and scheming had made him so distrustful. He began tentatively, telling part of the story, hiding his famous identity. Other members of the court tested his words, displaying insatiable Greek curiosity. They tried to discover just who he was and if he told the truth. The first night they feasted.

The next day Alcinous called for competitive games: footraces, wrestling, jumping contests and discus throwing. When one of Alcinous' sons won the boxing contest he challenged Ulysses to compete, praising him, appealing to his manly pride.

The wanderer resisted. Suddenly another man, winner of the wrestling contest, interrupted. "Perhaps our visitor is simply not an athlete, just a greedy businessman, a merchant from a cargo ship."

Ulysses responded. "You're a fool. Some men are simple in appearance yet their words are reserved, clear and confident. Others are as handsome as gods, but their words are meaningless because their heads are empty. That is your fate."

Ulysses leaped to his feet, grabbed a large stone, spun and hurled it further than all the other discus throwers.

King Alcinous interceded. "Stranger, listen so when you reach home you can relate our excellent way of life. At boxing and wrestling we are not superior, but we're fine runners and we rule the seas. We love dining with our friends, music, beautiful clothing, warm baths and the bedroom."

Alcinous turned to the crowd. "Come, masters of dance, show our guest your skills."

Nine officials set off a place for dancing. A bard took his harp and moved to the center of the area, then around him young men beat time. The two finest dancers, sons of Alcinous, whirled and moved, their feet tracing out intricate patterns. Ulysses watched, enchanted.

The dancing ceased; the feasting continued. Poets sang grand tales. One told of the Trojan War, and Ulysses broke down and sobbed, hiding his grief from the crowd. No one but Alcinous was aware of his sorrow. The king made the poet stop and begged Ulysses to tell his whole story. Finally surrendering to their sincerity, Ulysses relented, revealed his identity and told the story of his ten years of wandering and adventure.

Spellbound, the court of Alcinous listened. The day drew to a close and Ulysses finished. The seamen of Corfu, their curiosity satisfied, prepared a swift ship. With Ulysses and his gifts as cargo they set sail toward Ithaca.

Ulysses had received more genuine kindness and hospitality in his first forty-eight hours back in Greece than in twenty years outside the country.

All night long the ship sped south. The next day they reached the rocky island, and the sailors deposited the sleeping hero on a misty beach then slipped away. Ulysses awoke.

The fog was thick. So many years of suspicion made him wonder if even Alcinous had tricked him. The sun

warmed the air, the fog dissipated and slowly he realized
... *he was home. At last!*

Many people would break down and weep, then
run home anxious to embrace family and friends.
Ulysses' reaction showed why he survived so much
tribulation and why warriors like Achilles died. He kept
his passions in check. No one loved his home more than
Ulysses. No one could be more anxious to discover if his
wife and father were alive, to see a twenty-year-old son
he had abandoned as an infant.

Ulysses found his old shepherd, a servant named
Eumaeus. He found his son. He enlisted his old nurse
and a faithful cowherd. Disguised as a beggar he
infiltrated the palace, filled with greedy suitors anxious
for Penelope's hand.

Penelope had stalled for time. She announced she
would select one of the suitors after finishing an
elaborate tapestry. She worked on that tapestry every
day. Each night she secretly undid the day's work. The
tapestry was never finished.

Ulysses circulated around his home. Patiently he
tested loyalties. At the right moment, aided by his son
and the three faithful slaves, Ulysses rose and struck
without mercy, slaughtering every intruder.

In the Homeric era slavery existed in Greece, but it
was not as widespread as in other lands. Servants were
sometimes treated badly, but they were often treated
very well. Eurybates the herald, Eurycleia the nurse,
Eumaeus the swineherd and the handmaids of Nausicaa
were not handled as property. They had their place in the
family unit. That innate belief in the closeness of the gods
and the importance of the individual filtered through all
aspects of Greek life.

Ulysses has enchanted people for millennia. He was a man who knew tremendous challenges and great victories. He also knew agonizing despair and defeat. In the end Ulysses emerged victorious because he endured and used all his skills to the maximum. He resurrected his life.

# Part Two

Ulysses lived with Penelope on Ithaca the rest of his days. They watched Telemachus blossom into full manhood. Ulysses grew old and eventually his mind and body died.

Our bodies are very real to us, and our minds are constantly with us. Our spirits are much more puzzling and mysterious. We grow up listening to our parents' stories, partially absorbing their beliefs. We watch the patterns of our lives unfold. The consistencies, the contradictions, the coincidences. We try to figure it out, devising theories about our spirit. What is it? What makes it grow? Where does it go?

The mind and body of Ulysses died. But what about his spirit? Where did it go?

In my mid-twenties I lived in Greece for three years. For the next twenty-five years, I continually returned to visit. I met a spirit that was different. Different than the spirit of the place where I grew up. Different than the spirit of other countries where I've traveled and lived. Different than my own spirit.

It displayed itself in attitudes, in personalities, in temperament. I moved through Greece, traced the footprints of Ulysses and realized that when you look into Greek faces, you see the past and you see the future. You see eternity.

Each man and woman is an undiscovered country, a landscape of thoughts, words and gestures contained in a unique body that is inherently Greek. And every island, every beach, every village is like a person, individual and special.

# Cephalonia

The island of Cephalonia is shaped like a large, high-heeled boot. Near the top of the island on the west coast, the rounded peninsula of Assos floats in the sea like one of Ulysses' boats, tethered to the mainland by a narrow strip of land. An ancient Venetian fortress crowns the double hilled peninsula. Swimmers fill a gentle cove created by Assos as it curves beside the mainland. Far above the sea a narrow, treacherous highway snakes its way around the edge of the mountains, leading to the most picturesque village on Cephalonia.

The small port of Fiskardo is perched on the northern tip of the island. Sheltered from the western winds, it was the only spot on the island not devastated by the 1953 earthquake. It is named for Robert Guiscard, a bold, swashbuckling Norman soldier of fortune. In the first century of the second millennium after Christ, this blond giant traveled south from northern Europe and spent the rest of his life forging a great kingdom in Italy. For forty years Guiscard fought and schemed and eventually united all of southern Italy and Sicily under his sway. Finally, in his sixties his eyes were drawn to that ancient magnet of land that once held Troy and now contained Constantinople, capital of the Byzantine Empire. Fascinated by the Greek world, Guiscard led his Normans east to merge that land with his own. He took the island of Corfu and set his sights on Cephalonia. Landing at what is now called Fiskardo, he was stricken with typhoid and died in the arms of his Italian wife.

Today distant descendants of the Guiscards, British and Italian tourists, return to Fiskardo every summer. Brightly painted pastel houses that seem more Italian than Greek face yachts that line the harbor. Past the port a tiny bay with a pebble beach holds several boats, a score of swimmers and a simple taverna.

Swimming in aquarium-clear water, I divert schools of tiny fish skimming over smooth stones below me. Drying off, I grab my clothing and walk back to my car. I insert the key in the trunk, and it snaps off in the lock. Now I can't open the door.

I rented the auto in Athens, and the agency has no office on Cephalonia. I walk toward the taverna. Draped with grape trellises, a courtyard of whitewashed stonewalls holds half a dozen tables in front of a small building. Cicadas buzz, and a sizzling charcoal grill fills the air with the smell of frying fish. The proprietor is Costas. He listens to my plight without expression. "I'll drive you into town."

Nervous and grateful I thank him profusely. He looks at me. "Why all the thanks? We're human beings."

In town I call the rental car agency, and they promise to have a replacement key on the first bus the next morning. It will leave Athens at 6:30 a.m., motor four hours across Greece, drive onto a ferryboat and arrive in Cephalonia just after noon. That evening I sit and eat a simple dinner at the taverna while tourists file in and out. Costas and his wife join me, and he chats about his routine. He lives in Athens in the winter and works this little restaurant during the summers. A black cat wanders around the legs of our table. Costas feeds it a tiny piece of fish.

"What's the name of the cat, Costas?"

"Gerasimos," he replies. Half the men here are named for Cephalonia's patron saint.

"First time I've met a cat with that name."

Costas chuckles. "He's the most sincere Gerasimos on the island."

Cephalonia holds its children loosely. It has always been a seafaring island. When the locals went with Ulysses for an extended stay outside their land, they started a trend. Today the summer homes of returning natives sprinkle the countryside.

Late afternoon in July my family and I sit in the main square of Argostoli, the capital city. Palm trees encircle us, the heat of the day has passed, and the square comes to life after the quiet of mid-afternoon. The sidewalk tables of the *pasticceria* fill.

The best translation for *pasticceria* is "sweetshop," but actually they are museums of fine art. The exquisite *pastas* are the handiwork, super-sweet pastries that dissolve in your mouth and make the ever-present cool glass of water the most natural accompaniment. The desserts are as enjoyable to behold as they are to taste. Master bakers use all their skills to create these treasures, displayed in sparkling glass cases.

Clothed like an orchestra member the waiter looks on while we make our choices. He holds himself like a conductor. Proud, erect, totally in charge of his realm. He serves without subservience.

We sit in the square as pretty teenage girls appear, heading out on their early evening missions. They are different in clothing styles and colors. They are similar, sharing a common dignity. In *Corelli's Mandolin,* Louis de Bernieres wrote,

> "There are more Cephalonians abroad or at sea than there are at home. There is no indigenous industry that keeps families together, there is not

enough arable land, there is an insufficiency of fish in the ocean. Our men go abroad and return here to die, and so we are an island of children, spinsters, priests, and the very old. The only good thing about it is that only beautiful women find husbands amongst those men that are left, and so the pressure of natural selection has ensured that we have the most beautiful women in all of Greece, and perhaps in the whole region of the Mediterranean."

Cephalonia is a big, robust Greek island, and Angela is a large, solid Cephalonian mother. She is sixty years old and she looks forty-five. Angela works long hours in her garden, constantly moving. As soon as she sits she picks up her knitting. "When the feet stop, the hands start."

Her village is tiny Defarnata, perched atop the highest northern peak of the island where dramatic limestone cliffs dive into the sea. Like flies on a wall, goats move across the rocky face of the mountain, bells tinkling clearly through clean, still air. Far below Angela's village the crumbling limestone falls into powdery beaches, barely accessible.

Knitting her lace tablecloths Angela is unaware of anything else. East of her village across a narrow band of water lies Ithaca, where so long ago Penelope stitched her tapestry awaiting the return of Ulysses. Angela's children are her life, but she holds them loosely. Her two daughters decide to marry foreigners and travel far away. With an air of resignation she says, "As long as they're happy."

She has raised children all her life. When Angela was eleven years old her mother fell out of an olive tree and broke her neck. Angela became matriarch to five younger brothers and sisters. When she married she had already raised a family. She set about to raise another.

Her hair is totally white, wavy and full. Angela says it turned color when she was thirty. Shining with a thin coat of olive oil, her skin is thick and soft, the color of light rich mahogany. Greeks use olive oil for cooking, in salads, fuel in lamps, as a skin moisturizer, in worship. It has been a staple of existence since the dawn of history.

Angela has a delicate nose, deep brown eyes and firm hands. Dedicated and at peace with her place in the world, she loves her family and makes fun of all outsiders. She has a humorous ironic nickname for everyone. Her neighbor to the left is a carpenter, and every afternoon the air is filled with determined, explosive nail driving. He is known as "the Hammer." The woman living in the house to the right sneezes violently. She is "the Volcano." Angela's one-word descriptions pinpoint each person's uniqueness. She crowns them as special human beings.

Angela's children say she is a simple woman. Their friends say Angela is very wise, giving her children center stage, elevating their opinions above her own. She exudes love and an earthy saintliness, taking the background except when she criticizes her husband.

Angela has lived through world war, civil war, famine and industrialization. She feeds her children first yet she is the largest person in the home. Of her brothers and sisters she is the one at peace with all the others. Everyone returns to Angela.

She is my mother-in-law.

# Lefkas

The island of Lefkas is shaped like a gloved hand, index finger pointing south toward Ithaca. It is a large understated island. The locals don't stand out, and neither does their land. It is either too crowded or too sparse depending upon where you are. The capital is too busy. The main beach resort on the east coast is too full of visitors. The glorious beaches of the west coast are blessedly uncrowded, and the rugged interior is largely deserted.

Lefkas nearly touches the mainland. Like a large peninsula slightly severed from its roots, it is almost not an island. Like a father who rubs shoulders with the world to provide sanctuary for his family.

Just north of Lefkas on the mainland lies a small inlet that leads to a large inland sea, the gulf of Actium. It was here during the days of Cleopatra that Octavian secured his position as head of the Roman Empire by defeating Mark Anthony. Fifteen hundred years later another decisive naval battle took place in these waters. The fleet of the great Venetian sealord, Andrea Doria, was defeated by a wily mariner who rose from obscurity and became the greatest admiral in the history of the Ottoman Turkish Empire.

The Turks were outstanding warriors but average seamen. It took a redheaded descendant of Ulysses' race to lead the Turkish fleet to dominance. For a generation his name struck terror in the hearts of European sailors … Barbarossa, *Red Beard*.

He was born on the Greek island of Lesbos. His father was a janissary, a member of the elite Turkish military corps composed of Christian males taken from their families in childhood, forcibly converted to Islam and raised to serve the sultan. Barbarossa's father retired from the army, moved to Lesbos and married the widow of a Greek Orthodox priest. They had six children, and two of the boys found fame and fortune as North African pirates.

When the older Barbarossa brother died in battle his younger sibling assumed leadership of the pirate fleet and eventually entered the service of the Turkish ruler. Ernle Bradford's book, *The Sultan's Admiral,* outlines his brilliant career. Like Ulysses the younger Barbarossa commanded a fleet of freemen, and he used his leadership qualities to keep bickering, strong-willed colleagues in line. His Venetian opponent led ships manned by slaves. Barbarossa outfoxed Andrea Doria in a series of brilliant naval maneuvers around the island of Lefkas, and Doria retreated to Italy. Barbarossa led his fleet back to Constantinople to a hero's welcome, and he did what victorious Mediterranean seamen have done throughout history. He plundered his opponent's possessions, looting the Venetian-held islands on the way. Throughout history a constant legacy of the Greeks has been leadership on the seas. During the years of Turkish occupation Greeks provided the backbone of the Ottoman navy and merchant marine. Eventually those mariners led their countrymen to freedom in the Greek war of independence.

In late summer my wife and I stroll along the waterfront in the village of Vasiliki on the southern coast of Lefkas. A series of large eucalyptus trees lines the harbor, casting pleasant shadows over café tables. Many who emigrated from this island in the twentieth century went to Australia, and these shade trees must have been

brought home from "Down Under" by a returning
native.

We eat dinner at one of the seaside hotels. Waiters
clear away the tables, and folk dancers appear. The men
are the prominent performers just as they have been for
thousands of years. The women recede into the
background. The music starts and the dancers move to an
inner beat, their feet tracing out intricate steps.

Today descendants of Ulysses dance all over the
world. At Orthodox Church festivals and Greek
nightclubs in America, Australia, Canada and Greece.
The formula is always the same.

The music stops, the magic lingers. I finish my meal
then exit into crisp, night air. My wife is at the hotel
entrance talking with the four dancers. The men who
moved and jumped now recline on the steps, smoking.
Instead of dance costumes they wear boring men's
clothing.

The young girls who served as a backdrop to the
dancing have been transformed into radiant, glamorous
women clothed in exciting female fashions. While
performing their hair was bound up and hidden in cloth
headpieces. Now thick, beautiful curls cascade down past
their shoulders. Eyes dancing, they talk with my wife as
the men silently look on.

The next day my family and I drive over the
mountains heading for Porto Katsiki, the grandest beach
on Lefkas. We pass through sparse, half-deserted villages
laced with the occasional prosperous homes of expatriate
sons and daughters who have sent money home.

We wind our way down a steep, narrow side road
with constant switchback curves. Scattered among thyme
bushes, wooden beehives line our route. A mass of

parked cars appears below us on a great ledge overlooking the sea. In front of the parking lot a series of makeshift cantinas hug the edge of the cliff. Yanni and Marina operate one with a grand view. We order a lunch of country salad and peasant bread. To our left, a series of vertical limestone cliffs like skyscrapers drop to a sandy beach that forms a walkway filled with sunbathers. Running alongside the sand is a broad blue boulevard of pleasure craft, tour boats and occasional jaywalking swimmers. Waves tumble onto the beach, deep cobalt color fading into ragged aquamarine as the water dissolves into the sand.

On the right, a curving peninsula shaped like a goat's rear leg jabs into the sea. The name Porto Katsiki sounds glamorous to foreigners. "Goat Port" is earthy Greek.

Two hundred stone steps carved from the mountainside take us down to the action. My wife and I spend the afternoon in the sea, swimming and treading water. We rise and fall with the swelling rhythm of the waves as if held in the lungs of God. Our teenage children leap into the sea from thirty-foot-high rock outcroppings. We hold our breath, send silent prayers upward toward the island's patron saint, and secretly take movie pictures for whatever posterity remains of our family after today.

Yanni's cantina is a converted camper trailer with a bamboo appendage providing shade for tables. At the end of the day as we return to our car, he kneels outside the back door washing tomatoes for his next patron's meal. Salads in many fine American restaurants are not cleaned as well.

We drive back to Vasiliki. Coming over the last hill, the large gaping bay opens below. Hundreds of windsurfers skid across the water, sails weaving bright colors against the sea. The surfboards cut thin, white waves.

In the morning winds are mild, and beginners take their first lessons. The breeze increases through the day, and by late afternoon experts are whizzing along at breakneck speed. By evening the wind dies and everyone goes to a *taverna*, youthful energy spent. Shining from sunburn they eat and drink with happy conversation. Wine softens glowing faces.

Phodas is a Greek father who is quiet, cheerful and at peace with the world. His birthplace is Karya, the largest village on Lefkas. Like blossoms on a fruit tree in springtime, white homes dot the side of a mountain in the center of the island. The town square is shaded by massive plane trees. Locals not tourists, fill the outside tables of the coffee shops. Their clothes are dark and sober. They stare at strangers with unblinking interest.

Phodas is eighty years old and has the face of a baby with few wrinkles and all his teeth. He never had a cavity and has never seen a dentist. Over the years when he had an occasional twinge in his mouth he said, "The pain came, the pain will go away."

He sits in a back room of his home facing his garden. Blazing hot in early summer, the shuttered doors are open for any hint of breeze. Thin, almost transparent white curtains hang in the doorway and keep most of the flying insects out as the breeze gently blows through.

Somehow a large wasp has slipped inside. As it flies around a light fixture on the ceiling, I look for some object to swat the intruder. Phodas senses my motives, stares at the wasp and raises his hand like a priest giving benediction.

"*O filos mu,*" he declares. "My friend."

During World War II, Phodas owned a restaurant that the German and Italian soldiers commandeered. Old black-and-white photos show a gaunt scarecrow near starvation. His expression is stern and determined. Deep shadows spot his face, the hollow spaces of sunken eyes and cheeks.

Today his body and face are full of flesh, full of happiness. He outlived most of the soldiers who ate food that should have gone to his family. His once skinny children are now tall and strong, and he harbors no bitterness.

Phodas is my father-in-law.

# Zakynthos

Zakynthos is the "Flower of the Eastern Mediterranean." During the second millennium after Christ, the Venetians occupied the Ionian isles for four hundred years. Floating at the southern end of the Adriatic Sea where it opens into the Mediterranean, these islands stood guard at the entrance to the Venetian sea routes. From 1200 to 1700 A.D. Venice was the dominant trading power in the Mediterranean world.

Zakynthos enchanted those merchants, and their influence lingers. Here Italian romance meets hardheaded Greek realism on a floating orchard in the wine-dark sea.

The capital city lies in a sweeping, semi-circular bay on the northern side of the island. High above the town sits the suburb of Bohari. On summer evenings open-air restaurants look down through pine trees at a harbor of sparkling lights. Singers sit at the tables, strumming mandolins and singing the island *kantades*. People stroll their evening *volta* before dining.

Zakynthos seems unstable. Earthquakes have shaken it more often than any other Greek island. The earthquake in 1953 destroyed the graceful Venetian capital. Today new homes and commercial buildings rise in the unique *Zante* style with sprawling arches, like people using wide stances to keep their balance on unstable ground.

At first glance the Greeks seem unstable. They are a paradoxical and passionate people swinging violently between joy and tragedy, happiness and misery, love and hate. These universal dualities regulate the lives of all humanity. In Greece the pendulum lurches abruptly.

*Schizophrenia* literally means "torn brain." In the western world this term describes a type of mental illness. To a foreigner the violent mood swings of the Greeks seem chaotic, out of control, almost schizophrenic. They are not. Greek character is very dependable. At the core of these swings in temperament lies a singleness of character that is focused and settled. Greeks know who they are.

Zakynthos is dependable. Neither earthquake nor foreigner can alter its character. No matter the onslaught of invaders, pirates or tourists, this island remains little changed. In *Journey to the Morea* Nikos Kazantzakis notes that if unwitting visitors remain in Greece, they find themselves moved from a position of strength to one of weakness. They arrive with a sword or a sack full of foreign currency, but they are eventually overcome. They marry natives and slowly their social patterns dissolve, melting away on the hard surface of Greek culture. They are absorbed.

On July 15ᵗʰ the festival of Saint Kirikos takes place in the central plain of Zakynthos. Vineyards and orchards surround the small village named for the saint. Our friend Adonis leads my family to the local church in early evening. A dozen lambs and one goat turn on spits in the churchyard. Adonis urges us to try the goat so we sample the roasted meat with wine and *polenta*. A high school band strikes up a march at the side entrance of the church. Priests wearing black robes, long beards, and serious expressions emerge from the sanctuary holding large icons and heavy gold books in front of them like signs. They begin to walk through the village and magnetically a line of people follows, drawn by symbols of spiritual power.

We fall in behind and file through town returning as night falls. On the flat roofs of houses surrounding the churchyard young men approach fireworks propped against metal frames. They light the wicks and sprint across the rooftops as fire and noise shoot into the sky. A four-piece band sets up near the remains of the spinning lamb carcasses. Soon everyone - men, women, boys and girls join in the steps of various folk tunes. Our children take turns dancing the *Zeibekiko*. The Greeks of Asia Minor originally learned this dance from the Zeybeks, a migrant tribe from Central Asia. Unlike most Greek dances that are performed in a circle by a group, the *Zeibekiko* is a solo dance of improvisation. A lone dancer traces out steps to a dignified beat while his comrades kneel and clap in a circle around him. Locked in harmony with the haunting melody, head downcast, each dancer performs his personal variation oblivious to all else.

Countless other dances, some local, some national, extend past midnight. The Greeks supply endless energy but no showy displays or climactic moments of frenzy, just steady fun echoing timeless themes of dignity and moderation. Joining hands we move in a circle, locked in a chain of community and kinship. Finally the music fades. Adonis carries his grandson as we leave.

"We haven't had a festival in many years."

"Why not?"

"We tried it twenty years ago, and it wasn't successful."

Visiting Greece leaves a memory of attractive people, but it's difficult to know what is so appealing. It's not simply good looks. Some magical combination of climate, exercise, diet, personal pride, - and kinship with the sea.

Vasso is a citizen of Zakynthos, and she can spend hours in the sea. The day passes as she floats around, sun shimmering off water as smooth as oil. Some people swim for exercise. Some swim to cool off. Vasso doesn't so much swim; she floats around content as a child in the sea of its mother's womb.

The water at the edge of the beach becomes a social club where neighbors swimmingly stroll in an aquatic promenade. Gossiping, checking family histories, doing the things human beings should do but easily forget in a too-busy world. These amphibians bounce along, trading recipes, talking about far-flung expatriate relatives. It's a social gathering with no age limits, no bias of dress or social position, only floating heads whose hidden bodies gather strength from the life of the sea.

*****

Vasso and I have been married for over twenty years. It's late afternoon in winter, and we sit in a high school gym in America watching our youngest son wrestle. At home his bookcase holds athletic awards, replicas of silver and gold cups patterned on the trophies Ulysses competed for in the games at Troy.

Our son is tall and lean. He tries to outlast, outmaneuver and out-trick his opponent. The other parents sitting around us cheer.

I glance at Vasso. Unaware of the applause and noise, an unconscious look of awe covers her face as she watches the wrestlers. My Greek wife sits on wooden bleachers in a high school gym surrounded by Americans, but she is not here.

She's in the long distant past watching men like Ulysses compete in games that will become known as the Olympics. Eyes fixed on the wrestlers her lips begin to move. Four soft words tumble from her mouth, spoken to no one present,

"What a beautiful sport!"

## Near Egion

My wife and I are at a hotel on the shore of the Corinthian gulf near Egion. The hotel sits on a sandy beach overlooking the water. It is early August, and everyone in Europe is on holiday. The place is packed.

Here I discover the European lodging schemes of half-board and full-board. Half-board is breakfast and one meal a day (either lunch or dinner), and full-board is breakfast and two meals per day. No one worries about what is on the fixed menu. Everything served is excellent, eliminating all the complexity, extra conversation and delays that occur when ordering a meal. The separate courses arrive with your companions' meals, at uniform temperature and better prepared because a harried chef has not worried about diversity in food requests.

The glass doors are open to the beach. Sunshine, pleasant breezes and tourists stream through the dining room. The noise level is a happy buzz that aids digestion. The male waiters dart around in their standard attire, white shirts and black pants.

Outside a row of tables lines the veranda. The tourists are mainly northern Europeans. Most have little acquaintance with sunscreen. They are grilled the color of freshly boiled lobster.

One fellow is very tall even by Nordic standards. A bronze face crowned with sun-bleached hair. His body is an elongated "V" with wide shoulders narrowing to his waist then tapering down to the ground. All over this walking wedge sprouts body hair whitened to the same albino-like shade as the top of his head. Eyes squinting against the onslaught of the midday sun, his sole piece of clothing is a scanty Olympic-type swimsuit. He wears the garment squeezed together from top to bottom reduced to the merest band of fabric.

The afternoon slips by, and we drive into the hills behind the hotel. The setting sun streaks the sky with rosy rays, and slim cypress trees point like dark green arrows toward the striped, red and blue canopy. Ahead is the "Achaia Clauss" winery. The province is Achaia, named for one of the ancient Greek tribes.

When Vasso was a child, after dinner her father would give her a tiny sip of a rich, sweet wine called "*Mavrodaphne.*" She says, "When we were kids we thought it was candy."

The Greeks have a notorious "sweet tooth." Their desserts ooze with honey. Throughout the *Odyssey* honeyed wine was the drink of choice. Ulysses used it to drug the giant who attacked his men in Sicily. King Alcinous served it to the hero in Corfu. *Mavrodaphne* is the modern equivalent of the drink of the ancients.

Cypresses surround the buildings of the winery. We drive into the courtyard, not a leaf stirs. My wife springs from the car and walks to the main building's front door, built of stout wood like a cathedral entrance. She pounds on it.

The door slowly opens. A little old man appears and looks up at us. With a mild tone he chants, "Yes, my child."

"Hi Grandpa! How are you doing?"

"Fine, my child. What do you wish?"

"We want to see the winery."

"Come along." He turns and we follow inside.

A darkened hallway leads to the central part of the building. Beams of light stream down from windows above, splitting the darkness. Silence surrounds us as we pass huge oak barrels twice our height, lying on their sides. In true Greek fashion Vasso and our guide are unmindful of each other's moods. My wife is in a childhood candy store. The old man is a reverent host.

"Where are you from, Grandpa?"

"I was born here, my child."

"Where? This village, ...in Patras...?"

"No, my child, I was born *here* in the winery."

Engraved on the bottom of the next barrel are the numbers "1882", and I wonder which is older, the barrel or our guide. We meander through this labyrinth past silent figures engaged in winemaking rituals.

Returning to the entrance the little man faces us. "Goodbye, children. *Kalo taksidi.*" Good journey.

He turns and darkness swallows him. We walk to the car. I think about wine and worship, blood and communion, ancient barrels and eternity.

Vasso looks down. "I wish he'd given us a sip!"

# Driving to Corinth

It's springtime during my early years in Greece. I'm driving from Athens to Corinth, and I'm in a sour mood. This week I had what for me was a serious argument with a Greek friend.

Quarrels are a normal part of your day here, like breakfast or an afternoon nap. Now that I've lived in this country a few years I'm starting to think that energized disagreements are a necessary and healthy part of living.

American therapists talk about *"catharsis,"* the release of pent-up, repressed feelings that results in an emotional, even physical relief. There are a lot of bottled-up feelings and frustrations in America. That culture encourages values such as "not bothering others with your problems," remaining "calm and cool" in the face of difficult circumstances, and putting on a "good face" in all situations. As a result many Americans are wound tighter than a drum.

There is little suppressed emotion in Greece. Each day millions of emotional explosions pepper the countryside. Much yelling and screaming going on. Husbands and wives, brothers and sisters, Aunt Eleni and the neighborhood grocer. These everyday exercises in *catharsis* are oddly non-personal, quickly forgotten and rarely escalating to physical altercations. Assault rates are low.

Greeks are among the longest-lived people in the civilized world. Greek men especially stand out in actuarial tables as examples of longevity. In addition to all the other factors affecting health and lifespan, you wonder if lack of stress isn't a major contributor. Stress is not tolerated here. It is quickly released.

This busy stretch of road goes through an industrial sector full of machine shops, oil refineries, ship repair facilities and other eyesores. Out of town the road rises, the morning sun is at my back and things seem brighter. The highway peaks and the Corinthian gulf stretches ahead, flat and peaceful.

Groups of foreign hitchhikers dot the edges of the highway, young people dressed in slight variations of the standard budget-tourist uniform. Blue jeans and tee shirt, backpack, eating an apple. Passing two harmless looking young men, I slow down and stop on the edge of the highway. The two guys jog to the car and peer in the window.

"Where are you two headed?"

They glance at one other.

"West." The thinner one answers. "How about you?"

"I'm going toward Corinth." I reply. "Hop in."

The bigger one squeezes into the back seat. The thin fellow climbs in the front. I pull back into traffic.

"Where are you from?"

"Canada."

The early 1970s marked the end of the Vietnam War, and anti-American sentiment was high in many places overseas. It was fashionable for college-age American tourists to claim they were Canadian. It avoided a lot of tension and potential insults. The population of young Americans traveling in Europe seemed to dwindle, and all of sudden there were lots of Canadians.

"How about you?" The big guy asks from the back seat.

"I'm from the States."

We coast down a hill toward the Corinthian canal. The Roman emperor Nero tried to cut a passage from the Corinthian gulf to the Aegean Sea around A.D. 66. Since the isthmus is so narrow a fair amount of Roman determination and slave labor should have done the job. Nero hadn't figured on one thing. Solid Greek rock. His engineers gave up, and the passage waited another eighteen hundred years for completion.

The bridge over the channel lies ahead.

"I'm stopping just past the canal for something to eat. Which way are you guys going?"

"We're heading to Patras."

"Well, I'm traveling south from here."

We drive through steel girders as a freighter passes underneath, steaming toward the gulf. Just past the far end of the bridge, I turn into a parking lot beside a fast-food outlet overlooking the canal, and say goodbye to the two "Canadians."

Greek shish kebab, *souvlaki*, is the treat here. Small pieces of meat on an eight-inch stick, seasoned with oregano, lemon and salt. At a canopy shading a short-order window on the side of the restaurant, bunches of dark-haired pre-schoolers swarm around, chattering as their parents hand them shish kebabs. I purchase two skewers of meat chunks with pieces of bread speared on the ends, and walk to the fence overlooking the canal.

In *Return to Ithaka* Louis Golding notes that meat was prepared much the same way in ancient Greece. In the twenty-fourth chapter of the *Iliad*, Achilles has avenged the death of his friend Patroclus, defeating the Trojan hero Hector. Achilles then drags the mangled corpse behind his chariot, circling the massive walls of Troy, taunting his enemies.

Priam, proud king of Troy, walks into the Greek camp unprotected to beg for the body of his dead son. He pleads with Achilles and sadly relates that he has lost fifty sons in this brutal war.

Achilles is classically Greek in his interaction with Priam. The hero vacillates from savage anger to deep pity, from shared sorrow to sincere admiration. Each emotion strong and full of life. Finally he rises and sees not an enemy, but a heartbroken father. The natural thing for any Greek is to show hospitality.

"Sir, let's eat. Grieve later when you take your son home. He deserves your sorrow."

Achilles rises and slaughters a sheep. His companions butcher it, slice and place the meat on spits, then roast it. They set out baskets of bread with the meat and wine. Together they relax and eat with the Trojan king. Then Priam departs with the body.

In those ancient times Athens developed as the cultural and intellectual center of the land, art and scholarly pursuit reaching spectacular levels. Two business factors undergirded and sustained this leadership. First was the discovery of silver at Lavrion, just east of Athens. The mines propelled Athens into prominence. Second, based on this wealth Athens developed its fleet, harbored in nearby Piraeus. For a time Athens ruled the seas. Although the Athenians were a people of culture and intellect, they retained close ties to the land. Business was by and large left to non-citizens.

Located in a grand valley in the central Peloponnesus, Sparta developed in a military manner. Education was not encouraged and many Spartans were illiterate, but they had the finest fighting force in the land. Spartan women were among the most liberated in Greece, owning 40% of the property, running businesses, doing many of the things that their soldier-husbands could not do. Much of the remaining property was owned by the city-state, giving Sparta an early socialist flavor.

Corinth was the dominant *polis* commercially. For thirteen hundred years it was the wealthiest of all the city-states. Corinth straddled the intersection of the main trade routes and had two good harbors. It was a worldly city given over to business, and it thrived.

This system of city-states created strong allegiance. Even today when Greeks emigrate, they tend to cluster according to place of origin. You can travel from place to place in America, and often each city's Greek community has a definite home territory in the mother country. Brothers, sisters and cousins left their native land one by one. When they reached their foreign destination they headed for the home of family or friends, settled in and made a new life.

The Greek city-state structure also provided an almost fatal weakness. A mountainous land comprised of proud and competing city-states is almost impossible to merge under one political umbrella. The country has never been strongly united. Throughout history it lay prey to organized, aggressive foreign powers. Greece suffered much for its intense individualism.

Walking back to the parking lot, I climb into the car and drive onto the highway. The modern town lies on the gulf. It's a vague place. The prosperity of the ancient period has vanished. Branching left my auto climbs toward the ancient ruins.

A plain, dusty parking lot lies ahead. At the far end a gentleman in a booth gives me a finely printed entrance ticket for a few *drachmae.* I move through a covered walkway into another world.

The ruins sprawl across two great terraces, one above the other. The sun has circled behind a huge peak, and the ancient city lies in shadow. Like a large underexposed photograph, the ruins wait for me to examine each dark crevice.

A grand stone stairway, polished smooth by countless feet over the centuries, leads down to a wide deserted boulevard. At the foot of the steps is a small museum holding rare artifacts. Vases, statues, tops of old columns.

A stone slab with ancient chiseled writing hangs above the doorway of one of the rooms. As I study it the Greek letters merge into a comprehensible phrase, "Synagogue of the Hebrews." My mind spins back in time to when Corinth was at the peak of her glory.

Along the dusty road into town walks one of many foreigners who passes through Corinth on his way to somewhere else. Although he lives a thousand years after the Trojan War, this stranger and Ulysses could be brothers. Less than average height, muscular, with broad shoulders and short legs. The hair and beard are reddish, his face unexceptional.

Ulysses was a king who could sail a ship and work a farm. This man is a scholar who can mend a sail or make a tent. When he speaks he stuns crowds with eloquent, persuasive words. The king of Ithaca, Odysseus, became famous in the western world by his Roman name, Ulysses. This Roman citizen known as Saul of Tarsus becomes immortal as the Apostle Paul.

He walks into Corinth in what on our calendars is A.D. 50. The city is magnificent and wicked. A rollicking party town.

It is a teeming center of trade and business. On the hill above the city soars the temple of the armed Aphrodite, goddess of love. Pagan priests sell the services of one thousand temple prostitutes to Corinth's many visitors.

Paul enters this beehive of prosperity planning a short visit. He remains for eighteen months, living with Jewish tentmakers, arguing daily in the synagogue for the truth of his new faith.

The women of this era wore their hair long. They also wore head coverings and sometimes veils. The women who served as sex objects in the temple circulated throughout the city and dressed provocatively. They cut their hair short and did not cover their heads.

Some of the respectable women of Corinth began to imitate the temple prostitutes in dress and fashion. Using his eloquence, Paul attacked these worldly leanings as dangerous threats to the spiritual lives of those around him.

Subtle, repetitive advertising also drew attention to the activities of the temple. The priestesses wore sandals engraved with the inscription "Follow me" on the soles. This message was constantly imprinted in the dust. The main boulevard of Corinth was wide and busy, containing the *agora* or marketplace with shops, inns and other places of business lining each side of the street. Looking for a good time, itinerant merchants and seamen filled the taverns and inns. They drank from clay cups inscribed with the word "Love."

This decadent emphasis shocked the intense, driven apostle who saw his purpose in life as the spreading of the new faith. It was a religion grounded in the moral and ethical principles of Judaism but not exclusively for Jews. A force capable of embracing the world.

Winter closed in on Paul. He wrote his now famous letters to the Thessalonians of northern Greece. Those writings became the first works of Christian literature. Paul's subsequent letters to the Corinthians became some of the most controversial writing of the New Testament.

Paul spread a creed he was convinced would save souls. In less than three hundred years this faith became the religion of the Roman Empire. And this faith helped preserve Greek culture for hundreds of years under tremendous pressure.

Today the remains of ancient Corinth are peaceful. The bustling sensual activity is gone, replaced by a conservative society strongly flavored with Paul's religion. Throughout the ruins bright red poppies grow from cracks and crevices, splashing life among dead stones.

In the background a few, lonely columns rise from a ruined Doric temple that predates the New Testament city. The peak of *Acrocorinth* towers above. This huge hill has changed hands many times. The priests and priestesses of Aphrodite's temple gave way to Venetian soldiers who built a massive fortress on the summit. In turn those warriors surrendered the hill to its current occupants, herds of sheep and goats.

# On Aegina

Aegina is the island nearest to Athens.

Today despite proximity to the metropolis, Aegina is a place apart. After the war of independence in the nineteenth century it served as the nation's capital. Nikos Kazantzakis lived on Aegina during World War II and wrote his wonderful novel, *Zorba the Greek*.

The ferry trip from Athens takes about an hour, and the hydrofoil boats much less. Aegina town displays the charm of horse-drawn carriages and waterfront activity amidst aged, semi-classical buildings. Pistachios are sold everywhere. Purchasing a bag of nuts then munching them is what everyone does on even a brief visit to the island.

Vasso and I are bound for Aegina with our children. Our son is six years old, our daughter four. As the ferry pulls into the harbor we crouch at the front rail holding onto the children, talking and pointing at the sights. An American couple stands nearby, silently watching us.

We file off the boat, buy some pistachios and find a carriage for a quick spin around town. Vasso engages the driver in conversation.

"Good morning, Papa! How are you?"

"Fine, my dear." His eyes fixed on the horse hitched in front of his buggy.

"These pistachios are great! Where's a good place to eat?"

The driver slaps the reins and tosses his gaze toward a few *tavernas* lining the waterfront, as the horse jerks the carriage into movement. "Those restaurants are alright."

My wife asks the driver direct personal questions. They are immediately comfortable with one another. "How about you, Papa? What do you drink? Whiskey? Vodka?"

"No, my child. I didn't waste my life."

We finish the ride and walk into a seaside *taverna*. My wife and I order lunch; the children run to a small beach area just across the street.

Greeks generally arrive for a swim in the sea in everyday clothing. Seldom are changing facilities available near the water. Typically a person stakes a claim to a patch of beach and sets down her small bag of essentials. Undergarments slide off the body and emerge from beneath the street dress in a smooth motion without disturbing the outer clothing. Then in a similar way the swimsuit glides underneath the dress and is skillfully adjusted into place. Finally the outer garment is peeled off revealing a person garbed in suitable bathing attire.

At the end of a day's swimming, sunning and socializing, the process reverses itself. Sometimes a beach towel is wrapped around the body by male swimmers or females clothed in shorts that cannot provide an adequate shield from public view. A completely private changing room composed of normal clothing.

Why go to the bother? Why not place your swimsuit on under your street clothes at home? I don't know but nobody does. Perhaps it would make the drive to the beach just a bit less comfortable. The reason for taking the swimming gear off before leaving the beach is clearer.

The ancient Greeks elevated the human body to a place of admiration previously unknown. The emphasis on competitive games, exercise and nutrition was revolutionary. Their sculpture was an innovation in artistic appreciation of the physique, laying the foundation for further refinement in succeeding civilizations. Thousands of years later, sculptors and painters like Michelangelo sprang from this platform of reverence for the body. Their masterpieces were born in ancient Greece.

The modern Greeks are still wonderful caretakers of their bodies and health. Nutrition, warmth and exercise are crucial issues. Greeks never travel in damp clothing if there is a way to avoid it. The swimsuit must come off before departure from the beach.

After finishing lunch and collecting the children we reboard the ferryboat. The American man who watched us earlier joins me in the sunshine. We chat about the things Americans talk about when far from home. After a few minutes he looks at me and says,

"I couldn't help noticing how your wife talked with your children when we were docking."

"What do you mean? How was she talking?"

He gazes at the water. "She talked to them like they were *real* people. I just don't see that very much."

Time passes and the water speeds by. I glance back at him. "What do you do for a living?"

He looks over at his wife, ten feet away, as she talks with Vasso. "I'm a psychologist. My wife is a psychiatric nurse."

I've seen card games between old men in coffee bars come to a standstill when a grandchild of one of the players approached. That child received the complete, unaffected attention of everyone at the table as she spoke. Her grandfather listened as if she was prime minister of the country. His eyes were clear and alert, without a single distracting thought passing through them.

On the battlefield of Troy, Ulysses addressed mobs of savage warriors ready to plunge into dreadful combat and on more than one occasion swore an oath, identifying himself simply as "the father of Telemachus." In so doing, he elevated his absent son to a position of prominence. At that moment Telemachus was a child, less than ten years old and five hundred miles away. Yet in his father's mind and actions that son was an infinitely important person, his presence very real.

In Greece today things are not different. Every single person is important. Children speak with a self-assurance that many adults lack in other cultures. They have been raised that way for a long time.

# On the Coastal Road

My wife and I drive along the road from Athens to Cape Sounion, paralleling the route Ulysses took as he sailed down this coast on his way to Aulis. It's mid-summer, and the winding road takes us past hills sprinkled with the weekend homes of well-to-do Athenians.

Satisfied with a day's work scorching the earth, the sun relaxes on the horizon. The light fades, replaced by a soft blue-gray glow. We pull into a restaurant with simple wooden tables under a canopy overlooking the water. As we choose a place with a good view, a waiter magically appears clutching a plastic tablecloth. He spreads the covering across the table, securing it against the breeze with clips and an elastic band. At the slightest hint from my wife he starts to joke about whatever comes to mind. Every Greek waiter is your uncle.

After he recites the list of entrees, we ask to take a look.

"*Vevea, elate.*" "Of course, you come." We follow as his steps crunch across the gravel to the nearby concrete building. Greece is the land of the open kitchen.

The brightly lit restaurant is a beehive of activity. Quite a democratic place, there is no posturing or pecking order discernable. Everyone does his part and the barking statements are neither requests nor demands. "Yanni, the *barbounia.*" "Manoli, two salads with *feta.*"

Lobsters wiggle in glass cases. Like soldiers in formation, today's catch of glistening fish are lined up in rows on a table spread with crushed ice, their glazed eyes fixed in one direction. A large bowl is full of fresh squid. Strange appendages dangle from their tubular bodies.

Many travel books and magazines describe the elements and stages of food preparation. You flip the glossy pages, gazing at pictures of entrees with delicious sauces accompanied by the exactly appropriate wine. Those images are enjoyable, but they're out of place here.

Greece is not a place of gourmet restaurants or five-course meals. Robust living stimulates appetites here, hunger is the best sauce, and freshness of food seasoned with herbs is the main attraction. I decide on *marides*, a sardine-sized fish lightly grilled in olive oil and served in bunches. We stroll back to our table enjoying the evening air off the sea, and I recall my introduction to *marides*.

I had just arrived in Greece. After settling at the air base near Chalkis I drove into a nearby village. Circling through the narrow streets, I drew the hard stares any foreigner deserves and parked near a simple, whitewashed *taverna*. The restaurant was filled with older men dressed in dark clothing.

Plates full of small fried fish filled the tables. Beside each serving was a basket with half a loaf of bread, hard-crusted on the outside, beautifully textured on the inside, sliced in even cuts that didn't go quite all the way through. Like a hardbound book with a few, extremely thick pages.

A waiter approached and tossed a basket of bread in the center of the table, set down a water pitcher and glass, then dropped a curled napkin with eating utensils close to me. He spoke no English; I spoke no Greek. With grunts, facial expressions and finger pointing I conveyed a message of fish, salad and french fries.

At nearby tables the other patrons poured a liquid the color of apple cider from tall brass cups into short ribbed glasses. It had to be some sort of wine. I flagged down the waiter and pointed at one of the brass cups.

It was Sunday evening. The setting sun glowed over the mountains. All the houses, businesses and restaurants were the same shade of white. Sitting on the highest hill of the village, the dome-shaped sanctuary was the largest structure in town. Bells chimed; women and children made their way to church. My *taverna* was the local men's club.

The food and drink arrived. I watched the experts. One white-haired fellow was devouring each fish in three movements. First his fork cut off the tiny head, and he popped it into his mouth. Then he separated the body from the tail, crunching the larger portion. Finally as an afterthought, the tail was harpooned and met the same fate. Sips of the cider-colored liquid smoothed the process.

I wasn't ready for this whole body fish experience so I reached for the brass cup. Sampling a bit, I encountered a startling taste somewhere between mediocre Chardonnay and high-grade turpentine ... *retsina*.

The ancient Greeks exported vines and wines to their colonies in Italy, Sicily and southern France, laying the foundation for the western world's future wine industry. The liquid was transported in giant clay jars. Those containers were sealed with resin to preserve freshness, and the beverage took on a pine-like flavor. As the wine industry evolved, it became common practice to store and age the fermented drink in oak barrels rather than clay jars. Today oak flavor is common in wine. Only in Greece are resinated wines still popular.

Encouraged by overcoming my first dietary obstacle, I cut off the head and tail of one of the little critters on my plate, lifted the body and tasted it. Gradually committing to this procedure, I moved back and forth from food to *retsina*.

In some harmonious and perhaps primeval way the fish, bread and wine combined in a pleasing way. Distinctions blurred. My companions at the other tables looked less foreign. The wine and food worked their communal lubrication. The heads and tails of the *marides* began to look appetizing. Soon I was devouring those little guys as God intended, gaining maximum benefit from the tastes, textures, vitamins and minerals present in every portion of the anatomy. *Retsina* became the most natural drink in the world.

The memory evaporates and I'm back near Sounion with my wife, watching the dark curtain of nighttime drop beside the sea. Five young people dine two tables away. One of the boys is making a marginal attempt at cultivating facial hair. If he is like other Greeks, after a few years of pruning he'll have a busy job keeping a heavy beard at bay.

One girl is medium height, brunette, with dancing eyes. The other is taller, quieter, with short blonde hair strongly encouraged by peroxide.

The meal arrives and they go to work, turning food into happiness. The three young men share similar expressions, movements and devotion to the task at hand. The brunette joins them, moving right into her seafood. The blonde is not eating.

Across the water on the distant shore of curving coastline, lights of several towns twinkle like stars, each village a separate constellation. The blonde at the next table rises and moves toward the pebble beach. A small boat rocks in the water.

She peels off her outer clothing and stands silhouetted like a pale moon on a hazy night. Out of the darkness two black bands of swimsuit circle her at the chest and hips, the only interruptions in her glowing frame.

She moves into the water, legs melting into the sea. Leaning forward at the waist, she cuts into the murkiness. Shoulders and arms slice through the wavy liquid at a pace in harmony with her ballet-like performance from table to sea.

Chatter erupts beside us. The brunette has flipped open her cell phone, punching in numbers. She lifts the magic piece of plastic to the side of her head and speaks without focusing her eyes.

"Hi, Mom. We're at the restaurant by the water ... Maria, Andreas, and two of his friends ... Just finished ... I'll be home by midnight. ... Make sure you iron that blouse. ... Okay, I'll tell her. ... Bye-bye!"

There are few cultures so well suited to cellular phones. Strong family ties and an outdoor lifestyle create conditions for repeated short bursts of conversation. Like the automobile, the cell phone is an instrument of personal freedom. You seldom see callous use of portable phones in Greece. By and large they are employed with little grandstanding or loud speaking. Most people with a cell phone at their ear speak in private tones hinting of secrecy.

Greeks are great conspirators. They thrive on intrigue, little secrets and private scheming. Indeed the word "Byzantine" has evolved to mean devious and surreptitious plotting. Passing a businessman in a three-piece suit pacing back and forth on a busy Athens sidewalk, talking in muted tones into a cellular phone, you wonder what sort of scheme he is hatching with his cronies.

The brunette doesn't plot coups or power struggles. Her cellular phone keeps her in instant, intimate contact with Mom, Dad, Uncle George and Grandma. The family ties that drove Ulysses back to his wife and son endure. If they didn't have cell phones the Greeks would find another way to stay in contact. They always have.

The blonde emerges from the blackness, water dripping from arms and wet strands of hair. She's now a singular creature more concerned with gliding alone through the sea on a moonlit night than with eating among friends. She towels off, slips into her loose clothing and walks back to the table. Once again she is ordinary.

Sometimes when you take photographs of people ... friends, strangers, random acquaintances ... it's a marvel when the developed pictures arrive. Often a snapshot of what seemed like an attractive man or woman results in a very ordinary person looking out from the glossy square. The concept of physical attractiveness is deceiving and incomplete. Beauty is bound with personal presence, vitality, sense of self, emotions, setting, mental keenness, poise and other elements impossible to pinpoint. Outward appearance is one small chapter in a long complex book.

Ulysses was not handsome, and I'm suspicious that Penelope didn't turn many heads on the beach either. They were attractive to one another in other ways.

*****

I watch him for three summers. The aging body of a life-long athlete. He roams the beach, golden brown tan contrasting sharply with snow-white hair and the pale sand. Finally in the third year I ask my wife to go and tell him how much I admire him from afar. Stammatis becomes our instant friend. A champion beach volleyball player still active at sixty-three years. His eyes clear and alert, the three of us talk in chest-high water, waves lapping against us. Almost imperceptibly we begin to rotate in a circle, facing each other, no break in conversation. We move counter-clockwise in the same way that Greeks have always joined hands, faced one another and rotated in counter-clockwise cycles of folk dancing, mirroring the nighttime spiral of the stars.

## Swimming with Minos at Aulis

I'm swimming with my friend Minos near Aulis. One could never guess this is where the massive fleet assembled and launched for Troy. Today it is a quiet, uncrowded stretch of beach.

My friend is in his mid-forties, a lieutenant in the Greek air force. Minos is from Crete; he's named for the civilization that blossomed there five thousand years ago. The Mycenaeans challenged the Minoans, then the Cretan empire mysteriously faded during a period of earthquakes and political upheaval. Today ruins of the ancient palace of Knossos, marvelous and unique in design, remain on Crete echoing the memory of an aristocratic, feminine culture.

Minos breaststrokes toward the island of Evia, floating before us. The back of his head moves away until the dark hair is barely visible. Just when he is about to disappear into the thick blue soup, he turns and heads back, face growing larger. Dark dots of eyes, then a nose and mouth, finally a wide grin appears.

He swims until the last possible moment, rises from the water and that proud contented smile never flickers as the water streams off him. Sitting on the shore his breathing is as shallow and regular as the moment he first entered the sea.

A week later I am at Minos' home in Athens. His wife, Maria, is significantly younger than he. A tall pleasant woman, she moves with purpose in the background. Her two young sons are constantly in motion, but they never seem noisy despite all their energy. Minos presides over his realm with regal confidence. The entire meal arrives all at once, no sequence of courses.

We attack. The table groaning under the weight of multitudes of dishes bears up under our determined advance: utensils hitting plates, dishes passing, glasses of beer, wine and soft drinks clinking. After the initial assault we pause, regroup and attack again with increased conversation. The momentum shifts to full stomachs and empty table.

A large salad bowl in the center of the table becomes a communal focus. Each of us breaks off chunks of bread, swirling them in the mix of olive oil and spices at the bottom of the bowl. The peace of accomplishment descends as the sun sets; the conversation evaporates.

My host looks at me, eyes twinkling. "You like Greek coffee?"

I've been warned about this stuff. Thick, pitch black, strong and sweet. It comes in tiny cups. Two-thirds liquid, one third black silt. Seldom has so much power been distilled into such a small space.

"*Ne, efharisto.*" "Yes, thank you." Defeated by the meal, I haven't the willpower to say no. On silent, telepathic cue Maria disappears into the kitchen to work her alchemy.

In a few minutes she reenters with a tray holding small portions of black rocket fuel. After drinking the liquid I discover the mud filling the bottom of the cup. The coffee is about an ounce per serving. After a typical meal there's no space in one's stomach for anything more.

After the table is cleared we pile into my car. Minos sits in the front passenger seat with the smallest child on his lap. Maria climbs in the back with the older boy. We head into the hills north of the city, twisting up and down narrow two-lane roads paved with a mixture of asphalt and crushed marble. Tiny white shrines mark every hairpin turn, the fateful spots where unfortunate motorists met their ends in auto accidents. The shrines are small, windowed boxes where family members keep oil-fed lamps burning in memory of those departed loved ones. We pull beside a lake not far from the plains of Marathon.

My car spills its occupants. Minos' two boys run up and whisper something to their father. He points at some nearby bushes. The two little guys hustle behind the foliage, stop, widen their stances and fumble with the front of their pants.

Minos realizes I'm not accustomed to public urination. He smiles while looking at his two budding fountains and says, "They are pissink, Davess."

We reenter the auto and head toward the sea. Coming down the side of a hill as night falls, I see points of light outlining the shore. With windows open, air streaming in and hearty voices singing folk tunes, something whizzes past my ear and thuds on the rear glass of the car.

A startled driver, kids screaming like fire trucks, and the most excitement I've ever seen in the mother. I screech on the brakes, swerving to the edge of the road. Minos stretches his tall frame back through the confusion and grabs something from the rear ledge.

"Look," he says, "it's a little bird!"

I gaze into the palm of his hand. There held securely by my friend's strong fingers is a tiny startled owl, saucer-like eyes staring in wonder at the giants all around it.

"Davess, we call this '*kou-kou-vay-ia*'." He pauses. "I don't know the word in English."

"Owl."

His eyes narrow while his lips form a circle. Poised to shot put the word from his mouth, he can't dislodge it from the back of this throat.

"Aah."

"O – W – L." I spell it in English.

"Oowwlll," he stretches the sound out. "Difficult to say."

*Difficult!* I think. *A three-letter, one-syllable English word for an eleven-letter, four-syllable Greek word?*

With an obvious resolve to adopt the little critter Minos clutches its tiny feet, hand resting on his son's leg. This unleashes another blast of youthful screeching that Minos extinguishes with a blanket of soft words. The owl's tiny head rotates, sweeping the inside of the car. The youngster and his small companion look equally bewildered.

I turn the ignition key and ease onto the pavement, wary of additional errant birds. The owl spins its head and eyes like a lighthouse beacon on the promontory of the boy's bare knee. After a few miles conversation begins, picking up tempo.

A bloodcurdling wail erupts from the boy holding the owl.

*My God! What now?* I hit the brakes again. Minos' face points toward his son's leg. The bird has shit on its new host.

The child has the mournful air of a relative leaving a funeral home. Minos asks his wife to produce an appropriate article to clean up the mess, totally confident she possesses something suitable. Instantly some material is passed forward to sop up the disaster. As Minos completes latrine duty, my auto approaches the seaside village. The car is suddenly very confining.

We drive up the main street to the water. This small town is near the ancient settlement of Graea. Along the edge of the sea are *tavernas,* sweetshops and fancy restaurants, well-lit and buzzing with activity. We pull to a stop along the sand. Minos and his brood, minus the owl who has thankfully vanished, stream from the car. The boys race off, and we make our way to the nearest table. Minos leans over and whispers in a conspiratorial tone, "The specialty of this place is *galaktoboureko.*"

I look over my shoulder certain there is a spy about, hoping to steal this valuable piece of information. All those around us look absorbed in their own affairs. Minos has been teaching me some of the language so he repeats slowly, clearly and above all, quietly.

"*Ga-lak-to-bour-e-ko.* It means something like … milk-pie."

I taste the dessert, and it's wonderful. All of a sudden I have a strong desire to keep Minos' secret just between the two of us.

## On Skiathos with Yorgho

I'm young and single, riding a ferryboat from St. Constantine on the east coast to the island of Skiathos. While I sit on a coil of rope and talk with two American men, two females distract me.

The first is a young British blonde. The second is a trim, middle-aged Greek woman with a deeply lined face. Dressed simply and well, she wears strong colors harmonizing with her skin tone, blouse and skirt artfully wrapped around her. She speaks to several friends like a passionate politician trying to excite an uncommitted crowd, her cigarette lunging back and forth like a conductor's baton.

In the ancient past the Greeks invented real drama and built huge marble amphitheatres with remarkable acoustics, models for the present day. Edith Hamilton said there have been only four great writers of tragedy in world history, Shakespeare and three ancient Greeks. Great tragedy sprang from great life.

I look at my two male acquaintances and wonder that they aren't interested in the woman's performance, or the blonde for that matter. One fellow speaks, his hand drops ever so naturally to his friend's knee, and light bulbs go off in my brain.

The ferry pulls into the harbor of Skiathos. The two homosexual guys wave good-bye and invite me for a drink this evening in the harbor. The blonde's name is Cristina. She came to visit a friend but she doesn't speak Greek, and she doesn't know quite where he lives.

We make our way along the pier past old cannons, boats and tourists. At the first café a tall, slim fellow with a ponytail sits at a table. He nurses an ouzo and seems an

expert in economizing movement. I ask directions for
Cristina. He looks directly into my eyes and says,

"Don't worry. Sit and have a drink. You are on my
island now. You relax."

Cristina departs. I take a second look and sit down.
His name is Yorgho. He orders two ouzos, settles back
and lights an unfiltered cigarette. Inhaling deeply, his
eyes half close, smoke curling from his nostrils.
Downwind of the cigarette, the smell nearly knocks me
sideways.

Minimally arching his eyebrows in the direction of
the departing blonde, Yorgho sighs. "Is that your
woman?"

"No, just someone from the ferry-boat."

"Ah, there are many like her," he intones with
practiced boredom. "They come all the time."

During the 1970s and 80s, foreign women swarmed
Greece during summer searching for sun, relaxation and
romance. Many harbored fantasies of an idyllic
experience with a virile lover, patterned on the model of
an ancient god. What they found were young unattached
Greek men quite willing to practice their physical
prowess with foreigners. These male paragons of
pleasure became known as *kamaki*, harpoons. In the 90s,
although foreigners continued to arrive the influence of
the *kamaki* lessened. Female liberation came late to
Greece but it did come, and as young Greek men found
their sisters' friends more available, their appetite for
foreigners waned.

The ouzos arrive. I sip the licorice-flavored liquor
and it filters down my throat, blazing a path through my
chest.

"Yorgho, what do you do?"

"What do I do? Many things. I fish, I play cards, I sing. Ah, … and I play the bouzouki. The best partner. No demands. Very beautiful."

"I mean what do you do for a living?"

He looks at me oddly then his eyes roll upward. "Oh, I understand." He views me sharply. "You're American aren't you? You worry about one job so much. Why should I choose? Last year I fished with my friend. This year his mother is sick so we don't fish."

I leave Yorgho and walk up a cobblestone street beyond the harbor, careful to avoid irreverently placed piles of donkey droppings. Villagers are outside their square houses, aware of the ferryboat arrival, alert for visitors searching for a place to stay. I pass a well-kept cube, and a middle-aged woman with dark clothing and fiery eyes shoots her gaze directly into my face.

"You need room?"

"*Malista*," I reply, the word for "affirmative."

"Come! Look! Is nice."

She turns and leads into the house with absolute conviction I will follow. She is built like a barrel and moves with the grace of a large farm tractor. She wheels left, slamming open a hapless door and flicks a wall switch. A simple shuttered room appears, holding a large wooden wardrobe and a single bed covered with antiseptically clean sheets. Veering left at the far end of the room she bats open a set of shutters, exciting several scrawny chickens outside that explode in a chorus of cackling and fluttering. Sunshine streams into the room like a cannon shot, turning the bed sheets snow white. The matron rumbles back to where I stand and stops.

I look at my prospective landlady and realize she has the best mustache I have ever seen on a Greek woman, and I've seen quite a few. Middle-aged Greek women with facial hair do not smile.

"You like?"

"Yes. How much?"

"Ten dollars."

"Okay."

Next morning I head for the beach. A few yards down the street my landlady, loaded with bags of produce from the morning's harvest at the market, bears down on me. She plows by and nods her head.

Harbors and docks on these islands are lively places. There is work for the locals, and visitors stroll or relax in cafes. Islands are not self-sufficient. Boats unload merchandise and fresh food. The dry climate heightens the sense of smell. Food has more flavor, flowers are more pungent and beer is more refreshing. People grab leaves from mint bushes as they pass, rub the leaves together then delicately lift newly anointed fingers to their noses.

Greeks wear sandals of one sort or another in summer. The footwear lacks good support, and the soles are often smooth. There are many uncertainties. Cobblestone streets, uneven sidewalks, narrow circular stairways, polished marble floors. Foreigners devote much of their concentration to avoiding pitfalls. The locals move along without paying much attention. Yet they never seem to trip or fall.

# Near Troy

I am in the Istanbul International Airport on a flight from Rome, and my luggage is lost. This is my first visit to Turkey, and I quickly decide I will never see that suitcase again.

I'm on a business trip with some American GIs to an air base in southern Turkey. We leave the ultra-modern international airport and catch a taxi heading to the smaller, domestic airport for our continuing flight. Our driver zips us to the next plane, his taxi surrounded by the city's evening skyline.

In the third century after Christ power was shifting in the declining Roman Empire. Rome was under increasing attack from its enemies. The eastern portion of the empire centered in Greece and Asia Minor was stronger than the western half. The emperor of Rome was Constantine, a brilliant intuitive leader who sensed a power shift and responded.

Around 325 A.D., Constantine made two dramatic moves that profoundly influenced the evolution of the western world. First, he made Christianity legal. A persecuted religion of the underclass gained a respectable foothold, and under Constantine's encouragement Christianity eventually became a dominant force.

Second, with bold initiative he moved the capital of the empire to Byzantium, a small Greek town strategically located on the waterway leading from the Mediterranean to the Black Sea. He renamed this village Constantinople. Just as Troy once grew rich and powerful guarding the western end of the channel, Constantine's capital would swell into a majestic influential city, overlooking the eastern end of the passage.

Rome weakened and this shifted realm became known as the Byzantine Empire. Although the first emperors were Roman, within two hundred years they no longer spoke Latin. Constantine's empire survived intact for over eight hundred years, partly shielding Western Europe from invasion. At its core, culturally and geographically, it was Greek.

From the beginning the Christian church was controlled by the emperors. There was little separation of church and state. The rulers claimed divine authority just as the ancient emperors of Rome had declared themselves gods. This caused problems. It was also a powerful force for the survival of Greek culture during the difficult second millennium after Christ.

As the calendar passed 1000 A.D., eastern tribes pressured the Byzantine Empire. At the same time Christian kings in Western Europe began a series of expeditions to wrest the Holy lands from Moslem control. Those expeditions became known as the Crusades.

In the 1100s, the Byzantine emperor, Alexis Comnenus, was in a difficult position. Barbarians from the north and east were attacking. Western kings were envious of the strategic Greek peninsula. Comnenus made a fateful mistake. He asked the European rulers for help against the invaders. Eventually the leaders of the Fourth Crusade came to Constantinople, but they didn't help. They sacked the city.

The Byzantines rallied and for two hundred years they hung on. But by 1400, Constantinople was a lonely island in the midst of a Moslem world. The Ottoman

Turks, flooding in from the east, occupied most of Greece and Asia Minor. Emerging European empires (Venetian, Genovese, and Crusaders) controlled other parts of Greece including many of the islands. Finally in 1453 Constantinople fell, and the once glorious Byzantine Empire came to an end.

Greece had been sandwiched between Moslems on the east and Christians on the west. The following occupations were oppressive and occasionally brutal, but one thousand years earlier Constantine had laid the foundation for survival. He wedded the church to the state.

The Turks basically allowed the Greeks self-government through the existing Orthodox Church structure. Those parts of Greece occupied by western powers generally followed a similar pattern. Greek culture and language, interlocked with the church, endured.

Today Asia Minor is called Turkey and Constantinople is known as Istanbul. Following the pattern of both Troy and the Byzantine Empire, the Turks overextended themselves and grew complacent. Beginning in the early nineteenth century the Greeks revolted and reclaimed their lands. Today the two modern countries of Greece and Turkey coexist side by side in the eastern Mediterranean.

Two things are marvelous about this saga. The first is the incredible, conquering power of the Ottoman Turks. Invading on horseback, they were nearly insatiable in their desire to expand. At one point they controlled all of Asia Minor (modern day Turkey) and basically all of the Balkan peninsula, including Greece. Their empire extended to the gates of Vienna in Austria.

The second is the incredible resilience of the Greeks. Occupied for four hundred years by various foreign powers whose worldviews were often markedly different, the Greeks hunkered down, held fast and emerged at the end of the occupation with their language, culture and religion basically intact.

To say that the Greeks have had a hard road over the two hundred years since modern independence is simply to say they are Greeks. Read the *Iliad* and the *Odyssey* and observe the bickering, quarreling and dissension. Follow the history of ancient Greece and see the city-states challenging, arguing and warring, never quite able to unite.

In addition the nation has few natural resources and sits in an unstable region. The major industries are shipping, which tends to draw resources away from the country and tourism that depends on the variable affluence of foreigners. Much of the remaining Balkan peninsula is poor and racked with ethnic strife. There is continuing tension between Greece and Turkey based on bad memories burned into a collective consciousness.

The taxi traveling from the international airport to Istanbul's domestic terminal is another time machine. It transports us from an ultra-modern, first-world facility of businessmen and women in expensive suits to what looks like a shabby bus terminal. Nondescript people in heavy, frayed clothing shuffle in and out of an old, one-story building. Heads down, they mumble in low tones and look at us suspiciously.

We pile out of the taxi, gather our luggage and move into the run-down building. After checking in, we commandeer a table in the airport snack bar and order pistachios and beer.

Many of my companions are Vietnam veterans. I have no idea what they endured during that decade-long war. Or how it affected them, mentally, psychologically.

Many centuries ago Ulysses and his men lived the horrors of combat for ten years nearby on the plains of Troy. I can't imagine what they went through either. They fought the war, played sports during a break in the action and captured women when Troy fell.

My friends and I sit in the terminal and talk about what male GIs normally talk about. War stories, sports, women.

## Wandering Through Northern Greece

When I first came to this country, I worked at a military installation in the hills one hour north of Athens. Our small detachment of ninety Americans was on a good-sized air base of four thousand men. Every weekend I explored the countryside in my little white Toyota.

Some of the most fun was to head for northern Greece. It seemed like you turned your wristwatch back a hundred years. Old shepherds dressed in black tended flocks of white sheep and goats. Primitive villages nestled against the sides of mountains. Ancient stonewalls separated the fields of farmers, and clusters of gypsy tents looked like Native American tepee villages.

I drive north on a sunny Saturday and on the right is a mountainous area shrouded in folklore, Mount Pelion. From here Jason and his Argonauts embarked in search of the Golden Fleece. Further on, Mount Olympus lies to the left. From the highway that curves around its sprawling base, the mountain climbs straight into the clouds, a fit dwelling for the ancient gods. Past the coastal town of Katerini the highway veers east leading to Thessalonica, the number two city in the country. Commonly called Salonica, it's about one-fourth the size of Athens.

The light traffic is a relief after the frantic energy of Athens. Cars move in a polite manner with less horn honking. Down the main street past several hotels and a beautiful park, stretches the university complex. In the center of the park is a rotating restaurant perched on a tall steel structure, like a small Eiffel Tower mutated into a mushroom. The whirling top gives diners a complete panoramic view of the city once each hour.

Salonica has a very foreign air about it. Less western than Athens, less English on signs. Turning right toward the seaside promenade, I find a wide strolling area remarkably free of people.

Beside the water stands the "White Tower," a squat medieval structure with an Italian look. A series of ancient windows ring the top, and under the fresh whitewash old, dark stains vaguely seep from each opening. I hesitate to believe what they represent, but I'm afraid I know. This was once known as the "Bloody Tower."

Driving back into the heart of the city I find the original street and pull into a hotel named the "El Greco." The reception area is dark and quiet although it is barely sundown. A middle-aged man stands behind the desk, a neutral expression on his face. I ask the price of a room, and he responds with careful, even comments. He hands me a key from a wall of boxes behind him, and I climb a short marble staircase to the elevator.

Greek lifts are three-sided boxes that zoom to your floor while the front wall of the elevator shaft cascades downward in front of you. Somehow I never get used to that.

The next day I hop into my car, anxious to explore what for me is virgin territory. In reality this is some of the most well-trod land in the world. Northern Greece is where east meets west geographically and culturally. It is the southeastern edge of Europe and the boundary of Christianity. This was the land of Alexander the Great; he led his army east to conquer the known world. The Romans marched through centuries later, extending their empire in the spirit of Alexander. The Apostle Paul brought the Christian faith of the Middle East into Europe here. Later in the second millennium after Christ the Moslem Turks swept west through the same area.

My car climbs into the hills, meandering through well-wooded countryside. On the outskirts of a mountain town called Edessa a small sign with block letters announces "*Katarraktis.*" I round a bend and see the waterfall.

For an American who took trips to Niagara Falls as a child and grew up watching television images of huge hydroelectric dams, this is a letdown. It's a typical, long dry summer, and a small burst of water shoots from the side of a hill. It could easily be a large drainpipe. I make a mental note to come back during the spring when the water is gushing.

Black, wrought-iron chairs with gaily-colored plastic webbing surround a small cantina. The only person in sight is a girl behind the counter with dark, wavy hair shielding her face. Tall and slim with heavy-framed glasses and warm clothing, she has that self-possessed air of a person content in her own small corner of the world.

Walking to the counter I announce, *"Mia Coca, parakalo!"* One Coke, please! and immediately dig into my pocket for some *drachmae.*

The girl doesn't look up from her magazine, but in a voice with a heavy Brooklyn accent she responds in perfect, bored English.

"That'll be five dracs."

Stunned, I wander to the first table, sit down and commune with my soft drink. I look at the bottle of Coca-Cola with its classic feminine shape recognized all over the world. The container has strange lettering. The soda is fizzier and tastes a bit sweeter than American Coke, but it has the same flavor. The best selling soft drink in the world.

I gaze across the parking lot at my Toyota, manufactured in Japan, exported to the United States and shipped to Greece. It carries me all over the country, and I have no problem finding spare parts. Looking at the car happily reflecting the warm sunshine, I'm unaware that my Toyota Corolla is destined to become the best selling car in the history of worldwide automobile production.

The car, the coke formula, the girl and I each traveled to this spot in the middle of nowhere from far away. I get a primitive lesson about a developing worldwide phenomenon. In years to come, in the late twentieth and early twenty-first century that trend will take the name "globalization."

It is a movement that many embrace and some dread. It homogenizes values and desires in a way never before seen. Its power comes from two crucial factors, one modern, the other timeless.

The first factor is global technology. Airplanes and telecommunication make the world a neighborhood. Planes zip multitudes of people between continents in less than a day. Radio, television and film spread powerful cultural messages around the globe. People separated by oceans speak to one another instantaneously by telephone.

The second factor is an ancient one that never goes out of style ... wealth. Those with money control the media. Their messages and advertising power make Toyotas and Coca-Cola global products. Coke becomes equally familiar in Greece and Australia. People in both countries drive Toyotas, watch American movies and listen to music on Asian sound systems.

Some dislike this mongrelization of values, apprehensive that diversity will erode into cultural sameness. Afraid the world will become one big, fast food outlet. And to some extent it does.

But a long, turbulent history filled with invasion, war and occupation have not ended Greek culture. Influenced it? Sure. Destroyed it? Hardly.

Today ten million people, a tiny fraction of the world's population, cling to a peninsula in the Mediterranean that for millennia has been a violent crossroads. They speak a language spoken nowhere else. A language that Ulysses would recognize, although he would need a strong refresher course after three thousand years of modification.

*****

Chris is from Kavala in northern Greece. My first exposure to Chris was when I worked at the American air base in Athens. My boss was a large, powerfully built fellow named Harold. He played college football in the United States and had a chance for the pros but opted instead for his officer's commission. Being in charge of an air base's sports program seemed like a natural fit for him. Helen was a Greek-American lady who worked with us.

We are in the base recreation center on a spring afternoon talking business. Into the room explodes a middle-aged guy with a thick crop of salt and pepper hair, dressed only in faded blue jeans. Masses of black chest hair bursting above his pants, he walks straight to

Helen, looks at her with the clear eyes of a five-year-old and asks, "You have some quarters?"

Helen digs into her purse, produces some American change that this forty-five year old "kid" grabs. He wheels around and heads back toward the pinball machines in the adjoining room. Helen resumes the conversation without hesitation. Within a few minutes she walks back to her office. Harold looks down, shakes his head and smiles at the floor.

"Chris is just being Chris."

Several weeks later I am invited to the home of Helen and Chris in Glyfada, the chic beach suburb of Athens. They own a beautiful luxury apartment with an extensive balcony and a grand view of the sea. Chris greets me at the door. This time he wears a shirt.

During the meal with American popular music playing in the background he closes his eyes, tilts his head and bursts into song. After the dishes are cleared away our party moves to the veranda. Chris is reaching peak form. With an arm around my shoulder like a teacher with his favorite student, he points to the traffic buzzing by.

"You know Davi, if you took a taxi driver from New York and dropped him in the middle of Athens he would think we are all crazy, ... and he would be right!"

He continues, warming to his philosophy of life, "Do you remember back when your John Kennedy went to Berlin, stood up and said, *Ich bin ein Berliner!*' That was absolute nonsense. And you know what, they all went crazy and cheered! And today we can't forget that he said such a stupid thing. The whole world is insane!"

He spends the rest of the night wandering from guest to guest, slapping backs, laughing, entertaining like a king. Chris maneuvers through the crowd like a happy shark. His eyes settle on me, and I realize I will be the next victim of his hospitality. He moves in for the kill.

"Davi, when Helen and I were first married we lived in Los Angeles."

"You liked it?"

"No," he growls, pleased he can surprise me, *"it was terrible!* I used to go down to Mexico a lot. As soon as I was across the border I felt like I was home."

Around midnight the volume subsides, guests disappear with great fanfare and much cheek kissing. At the door I turn to bid farewell. Chris grabs my arm.

"You come back by yourself, Davi. We'll get drunk!"

Of course his intention is to shock me again. Drunkenness is not very Greek. On the contrary this country has the most healthy, balanced attitude toward the use of alcohol I have ever seen.

Wine was an important part of Hellenic culture from earliest times. It was safer than water. The ancients drank it diluted to a concentration of six to eight percent. Consuming undiluted wine was considered savage and unhealthy. In addition to physical problems, excessive drinking was thought to cause insanity. Wine was naturally consumed during rituals of sacrifice, prayer and burial. It was used to seal agreements, for health reasons, and during feasts. This essential use as a natural part of life passed down to the present day.

Modern Greeks are moderate "social drinkers." They don't drink alone, rarely drink without eating, and average alcohol consumption is low. During the three years I lived here I saw only two intoxicated Greeks.

One summer evening as we dined at an outside restaurant with my brother-in-law, he gazed awestruck at a man at a nearby table who had obviously consumed too much. Greeks consider drunkenness ridiculous.

Abstinence is also puzzling. Once I was on a weekend excursion in the mountains north of Athens with a hiking club. When our group stopped at noon all my friends pulled lunches from their backpacks. One fellow who I barely knew reached into his pack, pulled out two small bottles of *retsina*, popped the tops and offered me one. For no particular reason I refused.

He looked at me with the same amazed expression my brother-in-law had directed at the drunk. *"Yati ohi?"* "Why no?"

Americans tend to cluster in two camps over alcohol consumption. On one side are the party animals who follow the creed that alcohol is wonderful, marvelous, the fountain of all good times. The more one consumes and the more often, the better life is. Alcohol makes everything better. Business dealings, sex, conversation. The more one can drink and the better one can "handle it", the more superior he or she is. It is a clique the young are constantly tempted to join.

The other major American group is the "teetotalers." Comprised chiefly of fundamentalists and recovering alcoholics, they maintain that alcohol in any amount is dangerous, evil and irresponsible. Alcohol will ruin your life if you dare to dabble with it. It aggravates or causes marital discord, child abuse, illness, traffic accidents and death.

There are some Americans who stake out the "middle ground" where alcohol is okay if used sparingly. These people are less verbal.

The ancient Greeks knew exactly how to use alcohol and their descendants still do. In fact, eating and drinking are not separate subjects. They are one.

## Going to Spetses, Again and Again

When I lived in Greece I took flying lessons at the Athens Airport. My instructor was an American named Dennis.

Ready for my first lesson, we taxi our small Cessna around large passenger planes and jumbo jets decorated with bright colors and strange logos. A mix of European, Middle Eastern, African, Asian and American airliners tower over us.

Performing cockpit checks, Dennis picks up the microphone from the plane's dashboard. Using our call sign, the letter and numbers painted on the aircraft's tail (N96421), he pushes the mike's button.

"Athens Tower this is November 9-6-4-2-1, requesting clearance for take-off."

The speaker on the dashboard responds with a burst of crackling and popping, then a foreign voice with a heavy accent.

"November 9-6-4-2-1, you are cleared for take-off."

Surrounded by foreign airliners somehow I am not prepared to hear English from the Athens tower. My mother tongue has become the language of international air traffic. In the years to follow it emerges as the *lingua franca* of worldwide business.

We arrive at the take-off spot. After watching two silver beasts lift off ahead of us, I edge out onto the runway certain that jet wash from those huge engines will blow our tiny plane into the adjoining suburb. Miraculously nothing happens. I accelerate down the runway and at the appropriate speed, gently pull back on the plane's wheel.

Banking right we head over the water toward the islands of the Saronic Gulf, sprinkled like little treasures in the bay of Athens. The plane levels out in a sandwich of blue. Sky above, sea beneath. Speckled with clusters of white buildings and green pines, large pieces of land lie in the water ahead.

Aegina drifts by. We fly into the sun as it casts a glimmering path on the water. The mainland rises in dark silhouette before us, and the island of Poros lies just off the coast. Boats swarm in the narrow channel between island and shore.

We head toward a landing strip used by Olympic Airways to shuttle visitors to the island of Spetses. Like Poros, Spetses lies just beside the mainland.

At one point Spetses was my favorite island close to Athens. Sometimes I went on a slow ferryboat full of happy people escaping work and the city.

Going by air is a different journey. Watching the scenery ease by is like slowly strolling through an art museum, savoring each painting. The landing strip lies ahead. Dennis tells me to turn and line up the plane with the runway.

Landing is the most difficult part of flying. You must approach at a certain speed and angle, timing your arrival to put down on the beginning of the pavement. It helps to have a mental picture of what the approach should look like.

In contrast taking off is fairly simple. Basically all you do is keep the plane straight, accelerate and when you reach the proper speed, firmly pull back the wheel. The plane miraculously rises. Dennis has me perform a "touch-and-go." I descend to the runway, execute a normal landing then immediately accelerate and take off.

We repeat this procedure until there is some consistency in the way I do it.

After the last "touch-and-go" we climb to normal flight altitude, and I point the plane toward Athens. Spetses is to our right; the island of Hydra lies just ahead.

The two islands are like brother and sister. There are strong family similarities and stark differences. Both became prominent seafaring outposts from 1600 to 1800 A.D. Money flowed in as their sailors formed merchant fleets that roamed the Mediterranean and Black Seas. This combination of nautical skill and resources positioned Hydra and Spetses for an active part in the war of independence in the early 1800s. The two siblings jumped into the fray.

Hydra is larger, a masculine place. Austere and barren, its harbor filled with grand buildings constructed from past wealth. Spetses is smaller, more feminine. Low, lush and congenial.

Hydra was one of the islands that led the tourist boom of the mid-twentieth century. Artists and writers migrated there, followed by short-time visitors who made it a classic tourist destination. Spetses developed slowly, becoming popular with British tourists and wealthy Athenians who built summer homes in its pleasant forests. Several men from Hydra were prominent naval leaders during the war of independence. Fittingly, Spetses' greatest admiral was related to the people of Hydra.

Her name was Bouboulina. Her life began dramatically; she lived and died the same way. Her father was a sea captain from Hydra, imprisoned in a Turkish jail. While visiting him, Bouboulina's pregnant mother gave birth to her daughter within the prison walls. Bouboulina grew into adulthood and became the widow of two more sea captains, each of them killed by pirates. While raising nine children she took her inheritance and forged a fleet of warships. Bouboulina led them into battle against the Turks, menacing the enemy. She was a ferocious warrior who seduced her lovers at gunpoint and died of a gunshot wound during a family feud.

Outwardly, ancient Penelope and modern Bouboulina have little in common. Penelope was the loyal, traditional wife. Bouboulina was a revolutionary in a man's world. But at their core these two share a fundamental similarity of Greek women ... singular, comprehensive passion.

Each was single-mindedly focused on her life goal. Penelope was totally committed to her marriage to Ulysses. No matter how long she waited, no matter how besieged by suitors or how weak her allies, she endured. She remained centered on the man she loved, the son she was raising, and the institution of marriage. There was no other world for her, and no one could penetrate her world.

Likewise Bouboulina was totally dedicated to her passionate life. She exerted all her energy, resources and every waking moment to her path. She conquered a man's world without hesitation, attacking life, sweeping her foes aside, taking no prisoners. For her each battle was total warfare. She did not think of defeat, and she surrendered to no one.

For the Greeks, man (or in this case, woman) is the measure of all things. Even today every Greek has the certain knowledge that he or she is important. Each person's opinions are confident; his or her knowledge is conclusive. Greeks do not look to others for reinforcement. They speak with assurance, and they act with decisiveness. What other people do is simply not a consideration.

Hydra and Spetses are peaceful now, filled with visitors enjoying the islands' charms. War cannons are dockside display pieces, faint memories of a dramatic and violent era.

*****

Five years later I head to Spetses on a Flying Dolphin, one of the hydrofoil boats that have added convenience to island travel and subtracted charm. The sleek, passenger-filled torpedo bounces and roars across the water, aimed at the island. A slim middle-aged businessman sits beside me with several friends. He has a strong jaw and the dour expression of an aging wrestler who has performed well, but is wary that some new foe will best him.

I strike up a conversation about nothing in particular, the bland stuff that fills idle time. This is the second scheduled departure of the day, and I ask why he didn't take the earlier boat.

He snaps at me, "We weren't ready!" Signaling the end of the conversation as surely as a referee's whistle.

Spetses has a cute harbor square filled with open-air restaurants catering to British tourists. The Brits love Greece, and they come in huge numbers. History and sunshine obsess them.

I lunch with four young British guys on a terrace overlooking the harbor. Hung over from the night before they talk softly, eyeballs hiding behind sunglasses that protect them from morning's great enemy, sunlight. It doesn't matter. By evening they will be partying again, their recent misery forgotten.

I finish and leave them to plot their revelry. Walking along the water, the main part of town is an elegantly crumbling area full of early twentieth century buildings. The beach is narrow and swarming with people.

In mid-stride I stop, paralyzed. Ten yards away, sitting on the beach facing me is a young woman with the most beautiful eyes I have ever seen. The sea behind her is a glittering carpet of diamonds. Our gazes lock. All others around her melt into a dim, flesh-colored haze.

I break visual contact and stumble on. Slowly I become aware of activity around me. People walking, waves lapping, boats bobbing at anchor.

Each of us moves through life bombarded by countless sounds and images. Most of those scenes we forget. Occasionally for no really good reason, a phrase or picture burns itself into our memory banks. The carriage driver on Aegina, my friend Minos swimming at Aulis, this girl on Spetses.

Those images remain with me every day. In that sense I am always on Aegina, always at Aulis, and always on Spetses.

# On Corfu

Corfu is the island furthest west, geographically and culturally. It lies off the northwestern edge of the country. Its prosperity throughout history stands in stark contrast to the poverty of the mainland. Corfu is like wealthy San Diego sitting beside poor Mexico. It is the most European of all Greek isles and the only island never quite occupied by Turkey. The Venetians, French and British have influenced its basic heritage. The land is well forested with gorgeous beaches and high mountains; the capital city is a town of neoclassical buildings, arcaded streets and fashionable boutiques. A lively Venice.

Most often Corfu is described as sickle-shaped, recalling thoughts of fruitful harvests. I've always thought it best resembles the female figurehead of an ancient sailing ship, gazing west toward the European civilization born in Greece over four thousand years ago.

When Ulysses washed up on Corfu's coast he was welcomed with great hospitality by the island's princess and her parents. The *Odyssey* describes King Alcinous and Queen Arete as dignified and courteous monarchs. Those characteristics have changed little over the centuries. Despite overwhelming pressure from tourism this almost semi-tropical island welcomes its guests today. Many say the people of Corfu are the most polite of all the Greeks.

On my first night in Corfu I slept poorly. My daughter had severely twisted her back jumping into the sea on Lefkas. With her suffering in the back seat of the car and on the ferryboat, the trip to Corfu had not been pleasant. The receptionist at our hotel pummeled my wife and I with all sorts of disjointed advice. The public health service was terrible, but maybe we should at least go and get an X-ray. Or perhaps a private practitioner would be better.

A Greek doctor from the mainland was vacationing at the same hotel, and he was dragged into the conversation. He listened to our plight, then picked up the lobby phone and began dialing numbers. Without looking up he said, "I know an orthopedic physician in town. That is what you need."

He spoke into the receiver. "May I speak to Dr. Theodore?"

"Theo, this is Dimitri from Ioannina. ... Fine! You?"

"Listen Theo, there is a Greek lady visiting here, married to an American. Their daughter injured herself. Twisted back. Would you look at her?"

He turns to us. "You go to my friend at 1:15 p.m.

Vasso counters. "Can he see us earlier?

"Theo, can you see them earlier?"

He glances at my wife. "How is 12:45?"

She adopts a sad look. "Our daughter is really hurting!"

He mumbles into the telephone, then hangs up.

"All right. You go at 12:15."

Greeks must bargain about everything. We thank him lavishly and he smiles, pleased he can do his part in life.

I have no idea what this will cost. I load my pockets with American dollars, foreign currency, traveler's checks and bankcards. We make our way down a sunny street past businesses and cafes. A narrow alley leads to a wooden doorway. A spiral marble staircase winds us up to the doctor's office.

Several patients wait in the reception area. My wife speaks to receptionist, and after a short wait we are ushered into the doctor's office, ahead of the other patients.

It's a sparse well-lit room, walls adorned with anatomical charts, alternating with diplomas from Greek universities and an Italian medical school. Dr. Theodore is young with prematurely gray hair, salt and pepper moustache. He listens to our story, asking a few questions about circumstances of the injury, current medication and symptoms. After a few minutes he looks at our daughter and says, "Please lie down on the examination table."

He spends twenty minutes examining muscles, bones and organs, probing, asking detailed questions, having our daughter move in all sorts of strange directions. During the exam we chat about the time each of us spent living in Italy. Vasso tells him I am a university professor in the United States.

At last, satisfied with his investigation, he looks at us and says, "She will be just fine. Have her continue the pain medication she is taking. She will be uncomfortable for two to three weeks, then recover normally. Nothing is broken, and there is no internal injury. I will give you a prescription for a muscle relaxer."

Relieved, we thank him and leave the examination room. Vasso approaches the receptionist to pay our bill.

The doctor's voice shoots from the exam room. "Irene, come here please!"

The receptionist enters the doctor's office and promptly returns. She looks at my wife. "No charge."

Shocked, we inquire why. Irene replies, "Dr. Theodore says, 'From one doctor to another.'"

We return to his office and thank him. The Corfu nobility's ancient kindness and generosity toward strangers goes on.

Back on the main street we enter the first pharmacy. My wife exchanges the doctor's prescription for the muscle relaxer. The cost is seven dollars. I guess all the money bulging in my pockets was unnecessary.

Later we join my wife's good friend Aliki and her husband Costas. In a world of constant change and increasing homogenization this husband-and-wife comedy team is as constant as Greek sunshine. They throw conventional theory about successful marriage on its head.

Aliki is a bubbly person whose smile brings sunshine into every situation. She laughs and jokes from sunup to sundown without ever being artificial or forced. We can be in America for a year without a telephone call or a postcard from Aliki, but when we return it's like we never left. We step into last year's conversation without hesitation.

In contrast to his wife Costas seldom smiles. He was the chief engineer on a merchant ship, and no doubt he was good at what he did. Like Ulysses this guy never made any mistakes because of unchecked emotions. He is as placid as the waters around a becalmed ship. He constantly teases his wife about everything. Her disposition, her attitudes, her likes, her dislikes, ... everything. His teasing is an act without emotion, designed to amuse, entertain and assert his personality. He never gives a hint he enjoys his constant whining or the laughter it provokes.

Aliki and Costas are polar opposites in personality; their similarities lie deep and hidden. They believe absolutely in marriage and in each other's character. Their interests are opposite, their values identical. Opinions bounce off them without making the slightest dent. But underneath all the superficial jousting lies unquestionable devotion to the institution of marriage.

And that in the end is why this land is so comfortable. Personalities, opinions, character and relationships don't change, but they hardly blend harmoniously. There is always conflict, turmoil, and argument. You can depend on *chaos* and permanence.

We are at Aliki's home for the afternoon. Costas and I head for the balcony. He methodically stuffs his pipe with tobacco. We sit and gaze at the sea, and he speaks in chopped sentences.

"Dayvet, I was in America once. Worked a boat on the Mississippi River. It was summer. I was so miserable. We went to San Francisco too. That was twenty years ago. I came home, and I never left my country again."

Like Ulysses when a Greek is outside his country he is always homesick. In other cultures people away from home may miss the security of the dwelling where they grew up, perhaps the town where they were raised. A Greek's home has no walls. The beaches are his living room, the fields are his kitchen, the mountains are his veranda.

Later in the evening we gather around the table, and Costas holds court. Our friends tease him about his ability as a poet, gently pushing him to display his talent and entertain us. He dismisses the requests with a wave of his hand. "I really *must* be in the mood!" He acts reluctant, but he's really dying to show off a little bit.

Later during a lull in conversation Costas begins to speak, his mind rolling and composing. The bard's voice is melodic. He recites some silly ditty about Polynesians and pineapples, making it up as he goes. It has rhythm, rhyme and logic; we wait for the punch line. At the end everyone roars with laughter, and a rare smile creeps into the corners of Costas' mouth as he bows his head and takes a sip of *retsina*.

# Coming Home

A ferry carries me south toward Ithaca.

The sea is the great constant. Through their long and confusing history the Greeks have seldom ruled the Mediterranean, but they have always been its dominant inhabitants. Other nations have ruled land countries; the Greeks own the waters. Whether the fleets were Minoan, Mycenaen, Athenian, Roman, Byzantine, Venetian or Ottoman, the Greeks drove the ships. Merchants and fishermen, pirates and admirals, engineers and galley slaves, no other race has persevered in this way. Their survival is a unique saga of the sea.

The island of Ulysses looms ahead. Throughout Greece villages surround and cling to upstart hills crowned by fortresses remembering a past realm. In the same way Ithaca juts out of the water, its peaks evoking memories of an ancient kingdom. Walking to the bow, I look down as the edge of the boat cuts through Homer's sea. The words of the Greek poet Cavafy blow past me,

> "When you set out for Ithaca
> ask that your way be long,
> full of adventure, full of instruction.
> …
> Have Ithaca always in your mind.
> Your arrival there is what you are destined for.
> But do not in the least hurry the journey.
> Better that it last for years,
> so that when you reach the island you are old,
> rich with all you have gained on the way,
> not expecting Ithaca to give you wealth.
> Ithaca gave you the splendid journey.

Without her you would not have set out.
She hasn't anything else to give you…"

I came into the world in the mid-twentieth century, part of an upwardly moving, middle-class family. As I graduated from high school and definitely when I finished college, I knew that for an American there is no set, prescribed way to live. Everyone makes his or her own life.

A person can rise more quickly and easily in America than anywhere else. There are few obstacles and not many rules. At the same time, Americans don't automatically know who they are. If they are fortunate, along the way they find out. Some never discover themselves.

By and large, Greeks know who they are. They have retained that certainty through thousands of years of invasion, conflict and occupation. Their identity is constantly challenged; they continue to hold fast. They are a people positioned at a major world crossroad, standing stubbornly where Europe faces Asia, where Christianity confronts the Moslem world, where logic meets spirit. *"Looking west, but pulled east."*

Ulysses is the archetype, the ultimate survivor. His long Odyssey with its many "captivities" mirrors the history of Greek occupation by foreign powers. His victorious homecoming against all odds resembles the Greek war of independence. Today we find Ulysses in the spirit and lives of the current occupants of this land. Their physical survival is surprising. The survival of their personal qualities, cultural characteristics and life force is a miracle.

Take the time machine. Go to Greece and walk where Ulysses walked. Bathe with him in the wine sea and the liquid sunshine. Smell the herbs and sip the *retsina*. Watch the dancing and feel the energy. Gaze into the current faces and ancient souls of the Greeks, and instead of life rushing by, ... time will stand still.

## About the Author

Since graduating from the United States Air Force Academy, David Lundberg has worked as a warehouse supervisor, an environmental engineer, and a university professor. Along the way, he spent seven years living on the shores of the Mediterranean.

A prolific writer, he has contributed to the *Journal of Career Development,* the *Journal of Humanistic Education,* the *Journal of Technology in Counseling* and numerous other books and publications. He currently serves as President of the *Association for Assessment in Counseling and Education.*

David and his wife now divide their time between North Carolina and Greece.